LATINA/O SOCIAL ETHICS

NPLR

New Perspectives in Latina/o Religion

Miguel A. De La Torre

editor

LATINA/O SOCIAL ETHICS

MOVING BEYOND EUROCENTRIC MORAL THINKING

MIGUEL A. DE LA TORRE

BAYLOR UNIVERSITY PRESS

Cover Design by Nita Ybarra, Nita Ybarra Design
Cover Images © Shutterstock/Hannamariah, Neale Cousland, Glenn Walker (Mexican blankets: 3648230; San Francisco Mission Distirct mural: 12437056; stained glass windows: 28152061). The mural "NAYA BIHANA" is about communities taking their power back into their own hands, reclaiming what is theirs, and utilizing the natural resources of their communities, resources that have been taken from them for hundreds of years and that have made Europe and North America rich while keeping the rest of the world in dire poverty. Nepal was chosen as the subject for the mural because it is one of the poorest countries in the world and yet the people there are rising up to regain their dignity, move Nepal into a state of self-sufficiency, and determine their own future. However, the mural could have been set in other places in the world facing similar problems, including Latin America. "NAYA BIHANA" ©2002 (A New Dawn) by Martin Travers with Eric Norberg, Gustavo Sanchez, Pooja Pant, Paulette Liang, and Kaira Espinoza. Located at Balmy Alley and 24th Street, San Francisco, CA.
Book Design by Diane Smith

Library of Congress Cataloging-in-Publication Data

De La Torre, Miguel A.
  Latina/o social ethics : moving beyond Eurocentric moral thinking / Miguel A. De La Torre.
      p. cm. -- (New perspectives in Latina/o religion)
  Includes bibliographical references and index.
  ISBN 978-1-60258-294-1 (pbk. : alk. paper)
  1. Christian ethics--Latin America. 2. Social ethics--Latin America. I. Title. II. Title: Latina social ethics. III. Title: Latino social ethics.
  BJ1275.D4 2010
  241.089'68073--dc22
                                                2010020155

To the Latino/a Working Group
of the Society of Christian Ethics

CONTENTS

Preface   ix

I   Deconstructing Ethics

   1   Moving Beyond Eurocentric Ethics   3

   2   Moving Beyond Eurocentric Religious Perspectives   33

II   Reconstructing Ethics

   3   Where We Have Been   67

   4   Where We Are Going   89

Notes   125

Works Cited   141

Index   149

PREFACE

> *[Jesus said:] No one places a piece of a new cloth upon an old garment because the patch pulls away from the garment and the tear worsens. Nor do they put new wine into old skins, otherwise the skins burst, the wine pours out, and the skins are ruined. No, they put new wine into fresh skins and both are preserved together.*
> —Matt 9:16-17[1]—

A major problem facing marginalized communities, and in our case the Hispanic community, is that since childhood we have been taught to see and interpret reality through the eyes of the dominant culture. For those within the community who pursue scholastic endeavors, the success that is to be rewarded with a doctorate is determined by mastery of the predominant Eurocentric academic canon. Hispanic contributions to the discourse are usually dismissed as nonessential in demonstrating academic excellence. This is evidenced by the numerous scholars in the U.S. who have little or no knowledge of the scholarship taking place among Latino/as. The triumph of the colonizing process is best demonstrated when scholars of color define themselves and their disenfranchised communities through academic paradigms that contribute to their marginalization. Latina/o ethicists are forced to exhibit academic rigor through the use of ethical models that more often than not are incapable of liberating oppressed communities. These scholars are forced, in a sense, to pour liberative *wine* into the old Eurocentric ethics *skins*. To do so, as Jesus points out, causes the skins to burst and the liberative message to be lost. We Hispanics must pour our own liberative wine into our own ethical paradigms so that both can be preserved together and used by our community, which thirsts to drink this Good News. As José Martí, who needs no introduction among Latina/os, reminds us: *"Nuestro vino de plátano, y si es agrio, es nuestro vino."*

The view of the ethical landscape from the pedestal of privilege is radically different than the view from the depths of disenfranchisement. This book challenges the prevailing assumption within the discipline of Christian ethics that the present scholarly landscape, rooted in Eurocentric thought, is the pinnacle of academic excellence. According to that assumption, held by Eurocentric ethicists, the particularity of scholarship emanating from non-Eurocentric communities, as in the case of Latina/o-rooted ethical paradigms, threatens to weaken the prevailing so-called academic rigor. Voices from the Hispanic community may be needed to show diversity and political correctness, but they must be kept at bay lest they actually influence the discourse. The old wineskins of Eurocentric ethics are based on the presupposition that religion as a discipline is rooted in a nineteenth-century European definition of what education of religion should be. Even though our postmodern conversations may have persuaded the academy to reject such metanarratives, they are still enforced, determining who is "in" (academically rigorous) and who is "out" (has an interesting perspective but lacks academic excellence).

Excellence, that is, continues to mean Eurocentrism. Eurocentric thought, unconscious of how the discipline of religion has been racialized, claims to exemplify a color-blind excellence in scholarship for all of humanity. By its very nature, Eurocentric ethical theory maintains that universal moral norms can be achieved independent of place, time, or people group. Such ethical norms created by Euroamerican ethicists are accepted as both universal and objective, and thus applicable to the Latino/a milieu. To speak from any Eurocentric perspective is to speak about and for all of humanity, including Hispanics. For this reason, Euroamerican scholars can become experts in the particularity of the cultures of Other, that is, those communities that are deemed "less than white." Ironically, scholars of color have the particularity of their analysis reduced to subjectivity—to interesting perspectives that fall short of rigor, regardless of how meticulous their scholarship may actually be. Because whiteness is understood and defined as universal, the insights of scholars of color are often institutionally relegated to a realm lacking any universal gravitas. Nevertheless, marginalized communities of color have long recognized that no ethical perspective is value free. The subjectivity of Eurocentric ethical thought can be lifted by the academy to universal objectivity because the academy retains the power to define a reality that secures and protects their scholastic privilege. Reduced to a phenotype-based expertise, scholars of color are expected to dwell exclusively in the areas of study bordered by their race or ethnicity. Experts in the particular, they are neither expected nor encouraged to speak with authority about Eurocentric thought.

Reduced to and trapped within their race or ethnicity, scholars of color are geared to the particular, where they are continually forced to speak to the center, always attempting to justify their right to exist and the importance of contributions they can make to the overall discourse. And if a Hispanic ethicist were to become an authority on Euroamerican ethicists like Walter Rauschenbusch, Reinhold Niebuhr, or Stanley Hauerwas, she or he would be viewed as an oddity if not aping, for after all, shouldn't all Latina/os just study Hispanic religiosity? Hispanic scholars who dare to assess critically the works of formative Euroamerican ethicists face having their critique dismissed. The Latina/o scholar will either be accused of conducting a "thin" reading of the primary texts or be caricatured as angry. As tempting as it may be to level such a critique against Hispanic scholars who challenge the Eurocentric canon, it is important to refrain. Even though the Hispanic ethicist may be portrayed as lacking intelligence or simply hostile, he or she does provide a "double-consciousness" that is capable of revealing what those blinded by their privileged status miss.

As a corrective measure, this book will attempt to create new skins for our liberative wine by using the tools and materials indigenous to our "Latinoness." But before we are able to use our own Hispanic ethic skins, we must explain why the Eurocentric ethic skins are inadequate—why they will burst. To that end, we will read Euroamerican ethicists "with Hispanic eyes," seeing, maybe for the first time, how dominant groups have historically constructed ethics to suit their needs and protect their privilege. The first half of the book will attempt to deconstruct Eurocentric ethical paradigms to demonstrate why they are both detrimental to and irreconcilable with the Hispanic social location. When such paradigms bring suffering, oppression, and death (literally and figuratively) to the Hispanic community, they must be rejected. Nevertheless, the best of *mestizaje*, our cultural mixture, recognizes the European part of our identity and the ambiguity and irony this creates when we deal with Eurocentric ethical paradigms. Hispanics recognize that even what we should reject in our identity is part of who we are as a people. The challenge is how to delineate and reject those parts of Eurocentric ethics with which there can be no compromise or reconciliation (e.g., complicity with the U.S. Empire)[2] and move beyond those segments of Eurocentric analysis with which we can converse. The second half of this book will attempt to construct a new Hispanic-centered ethical paradigm rooted in our community way of being. The hope is not only to articulate aspects of how we historically have conducted ethics, but also to examine possible future directions. We search for a dynamic ethics that is not only living, but also lived. This is a Latina/o ethics based on praxis that pursues social justice, here understood as creating harmony within social structures by countering and correcting the undue power and privilege held by the few at the expense of the many.

This book is made possible by the assistance I have received from many individuals who believed in my task. Specifically, I am grateful to my Ph.D. students at the Iliff School of Theology for participating in a monthly book study gathering where we read the works of numerous Eurocentric ethicists to better grasp their arguments and propositions. This group of seven scholars read this manuscript and provided constructive criticism. I especially thank my graduate assistants Rodolfo J. Hernández-Díaz (RJ) and Timothy Sakelos, who helped me collect data. I am also grateful to Iliff School of Theology for a 2009 sabbatical, which provided needed time to write this text. Also, I am indebted to the *Asociación para la Educación Teológica Hispana* (AETH) for providing a stipend to write the first chapter of this book and present it at the Society of Christian Ethics in 2009. My administrative assistant Debbie McLaren deserves much appreciation for proofreading this text and providing crucial stylistic suggestions. And finally, Carey C. Newman, my editor at Baylor University Press, who believed in my vision to begin a conversation on the future of the Hispanic discourse, contracted me not just to write this book, but to start a series to make said vision a reality.

I

DECONSTRUCTING ETHICS

Ever wonder what happens when you fry baloney? I can expect puzzled looks from my students every time I ask this question. Fry baloney? Why would anyone in their right mind fry baloney? Still, I usually have a few students provide the correct answer: it bubbles up. It is interesting to note that the students who know the answer are usually of color, or are whites who have known poverty. Those who have lived in poverty, either as an act of solidarity with the marginalized or because they themselves have been poor, are generally the ones who know the answer to my quiz. For you see, only the poor—sick and tired of eating the cheapest meat available as a dietary staple—finally rebel and attempt creative new ways of serving the food of the poor.

If ethics is the construct of a particular type of culture, then those born into and/or raised within the Euroamerican culture are a product of a society where white supremacy and class privilege are interwoven with how Americans have been conditioned to normalize and legitimize how they see and organize the world around them. This racist and classist underpinning contributes to the metanarrative according to which those within the dominant culture develop their ethical perspectives. A worldview has been constructed in which complicity with the U.S. Empire is deemed normal and in which those who benefit from Euroamerican ethics usually fail to consider the racialization of their discipline. Few Euroamerican ethicists and ethicists of color attempting to assimilate to Euroamerican definitions of academic excellence recognize how the ethical paradigms they advocate are reinforced by a social location privileged by economic class and whiteness. As alluring as

Eurocentric Christian ethics may appear to Latino/as, most of it remains embedded within the empire and thus potentially incongruent with the gospel message of liberation found in the biblical text. Hispanic ethicist Ismael García is correct in characterizing Eurocentric values as based on "a culture that is dominantly rights oriented, impersonal, individualistic, and radically private" (2009a: 631). Generally speaking, Hispanic values, by contrast, are based on a culture that is dominantly justice oriented, relational, liberationist, and radically communal. Still, before we Hispanics jump on the liberationist bandwagon, we must also confess the difficulty of doing any liberationist work within the fabric of empire, for U.S. culture has made it possible to live with power and privilege and still claim to be a liberationist.

The shedding of tears by Euroamericans, or their expressions of righteous indignation over historical or present ethnic discriminations, mask the real question Hispanics should press Euroamerican ethicists to consider. The underlying problem with Eurocentric ethics is that moral reasoning is done from the realm of abstractions. Ethics is less concerned with "what you do" than "how you think." And even though some Euroamerican ethicists have begun to lean toward more praxis-oriented ethical paradigms, still the commitment to abstract thought more than praxis dominates the Society of Christian Ethics milieu. This chapter will therefore ask, why *must* people of color in general, Latina/os specifically, follow Euroamerican ethical analytical paradigms when engaging in moral reasoning? For to engage in the Eurocentric ethical discourse, either conservative or liberal, can be damning to Latina/os, even when the normative Eurocentric ethical paradigms are said to be progressive and worthy of implementation by U.S. marginalized communities. In short, can Hispanic ethical paradigms arise from the social location of Latina/os who know what happens when you fry baloney?

This chapter will attempt to answer these questions by employing a methodology that analyzes twentieth-century Eurocentric ethics to expose its indistinguishability from middle-class respectability and conformity, as well as its complicity with empire, and thus its inherent tendency to oppose marginalized communities. We begin our analysis by stating the obvious. Almost all the best-known ethicists of the twentieth century were white males. Specifically, they were white males embedded within a social location that informed, shaped, influenced, and constructed their worldview. Regardless of how progressive we wish to consider these ethicists, they remain a product of the empire to which they belong, reflecting the racism and ethnic discrimination of their time that continues to make empire possible. True, they may have challenged the empire, critiqued the empire, and even called for profound reform, but in the final analysis, they contributed to the undergirding racial and ethnic assumptions that provided justification for the empire because they failed to recognize their complicity with the overarching power structures that make empire possible. They call for justice without challenging the dominant culture's retention of its power and privilege. The end result is a "kinder, gentler" form of oppression. To illustrate this point, let's briefly examine three of the leading Euroamerican ethicists who spanned the twentieth century: Walter Rauschenbusch, of the earlier part of the century; Reinhold Niebuhr, whose writings were influential midcentury; and Stanley Hauerwas, whose work had a major impact at the close of the last century.

Frankly, I would rather skip the analysis of these three, or any other Euroamerican male ethicist of the last century, and dive straight into a Hispanic ethics of survival rooted within the Latino/a social context. Unfortunately, scholars of color working at the periphery of the normative ethical discourse are always forced to speak to the center if their work is to be taken seriously. To fail to do so is to risk having one's work dismissed as either unscholarly or irrelevant. Paradoxically, our very attempt to seek a different liberative path by which to do our ethical analysis simultaneously requires that we accept the consequences of Euroamerican imperialism and thus reinforce our subservience, even while attempting to reevaluate our ethos and its complicity with the dominant discourse. Our very minds have been so colonized that regardless of how critical our analysis may be or how aggressive a stance we take, we remain imprisoned within a defensive role.

The choosing of these three formative white male ethicists of the past century is not an attempt to disregard their entire work, nor is it an attempt to say that the ethical paradigms they suggest have no value. I am sure they have great value for Euroamericans, and I have no doubt they have greatly influenced and shaped ethical thought as done by the majority of today's Christian ethicists, many of whom are of color. Consequently, I am not calling for a total rejection of Eurocentric ethical analysis and those who originally formulated it. Obviously, some perspectives and insights from

Euroamerican ethicists can prove informative for Hispanics constructing their own ethical paradigms. Nevertheless, I am raising concerns about uncritically adopting Eurocentric methodologies for conducting ethical analysis, especially when those methodologies are complicit with the prevailing social power structures. I am calling for a careful understanding of the social context influencing their works and for replacing their ethics with one rooted in the Latino/a experience. Rather than reject these formative Eurocentric ethicists, a more adequate concept to describe what I am advocating is moving beyond them. But not just them. As we will see in the final chapter, I am also calling for moving beyond Hispanic ethicists, but for different reasons.

For most Euroamericans, Rauschenbusch, Niebuhr, and Hauerwas may very well prove to be formative for their social context. But the danger is to make them universal for the rest of America which is not Euroamerican. Although their ethics may appear very tempting to those of us entrenched in communities of color, because it seems to us that the survival of our communities depends on our acceptance of those ethics, these men's subtle, and at times not so subtle, unexamined complicity with the power and privileges of the dominant culture precludes our fully accepting their thoughts. We Latina/os must develop our own ethical Christian paradigms that are rooted in our own social context. If the liberationist's proposition is that all theological and ethical "truths" are contextual, then a Eurocentric context in which to do our ethics falls short of one rooted in our own Hispanic context.

WALTER RAUSCHENBUSCH

We begin with Rauschenbusch, whose eleven-year ministry in New York City's slums and contact with major figures of the social gospel movement made him one of the movement's significant intellectuals. The social gospel movement, which began to grow after the Civil War and continued as a significant ethical response to the social problems created by industrialization, lasted until the start of the First World War. Rauschenbusch was disenchanted with Protestant pietism and the otherworldliness it advocated, for it prevented the church from struggling to root the kingdom of God in divine and righteous forces here on earth. Additionally, he believed the socialist movements of his time were struggling for the kingdom, but without God. In response, Rauschenbusch attempted a synthesis so that through the Christian church, a socialist movement could be empowered to transform the world. By merging the church with the socialist movements he hoped to "[bring] them into their just and natural relation to each other, infusing the exalted fervor and power of religion into the social movement, and helping religion to find its ethical outcome in the transformation of social conditions" (1896: 203). For Rauschenbusch, "the essential purpose of Christianity was to transform human society into the kingdom of God by regenerating all human relations and reconstituting them in accordance with the will of God" (1907 [1991]: xxxvii).

Keenly aware of the social and structural nature of sin, Rauschenbusch spoke with a voice that resonates with present-day liberationist ethicists' concerns with oppressive corporate structures. Hispanic liberationists can agree with the preferential option for the poor he advocates. "When we learn from the gospels, for instance, that God is on the side of the poor, and that he proposes to view anything done or not done to them as having been done or not done to him, such a revelation of solidarity and humanity comes with a regenerating shock to our selfish minds" (1917: 186). Additionally, liberationists can appreciate his call for praxis. "Ascetic Christianity called the world evil *and left it*. Humanity is waiting for a revolutionary Christianity which will call the world evil *and change it*" (1907 [1991]: 91; emphasis added). But unfortunately, when dealing with the issue of race, he is quick to celebrate "the social supremacy of the Aryan race" (1912 [2009]: 376), thus providing a problematic response to the expansion and entrenchment of Jim and Jane Crow. Racial oppression for Rauschenbusch was a Southern problem that could be solved only by Christianizing the social order. For him, the transformation of blacks would occur through the example provided them by the white middle class. Dealing paternalistically with "the problem of the black man" in his 1912 lecture before the American Mission Association a few years before his death, Rauschenbusch stated, "For years the problem of the two races in the South has seemed to me so tragic, so insoluble, that I have never yet ventured to discuss it in public." But why avoid the topic of racial oppression because of its insolubility, considering he spent the majority of his career dealing with other insoluble issues that were just as complex? Nevertheless, he did call "for the progressive awakening of hope and self-respect of the individual Negro and the awakening of race pride and race ambition in all Negro communities. . . . the Christian way out is to take our belated black brother by the hand and urge him along the road of steady and intelligent labor, of property rights, of family fidelity, of hope and self-confidence, and of pride and joy in his race achievement" (1914: 732–33). In other words, teach the "Negro" to behave and act like Euroamericans, as well as to adopt white middle-class values and worldview.

His paternalism was not limited to Blacks. In several fund-raising letters for the German Department of Rochester Theological Seminary, where he taught, Rauschenbusch resorts to playing off the racial fears of potential donors, railing against the "blacks of the South and the seething yellow flocks beyond the Pacific" (Dorrien, 2003: 95).[1] He boasts that his German ethnicity and the ethnicity of the English and of Anglo-Americans are part of a single Teutonic "princely stock" responsible for creating, sustaining, and protecting modern civilization from "alien strains," like those of us from Spanish countries. In a 1902 commencement address given at the seminary in honor of the German Department's fiftieth anniversary, Rauschenbusch explained that "[i]t is Providential that Teutons hold the largest part of the world's wealth and power in the hollow of their hands, and the larger share of the world's intellectual and spiritual possessions in the hollow of their heads. They are a princely stock, these fair skinned men, an imperial race, as they stand at the forge of time and hammer out history" (1902 [1989]: 1–2).

Rauschenbusch laments a decrease in the immigration of Germans. "Cheap and docile" immigrant laborers from southern and eastern Europe "work against the common good" by keeping "down the wages and the spirit of the native American workingmen." They have "burdened [American] cities with an undigested mass of alien people" that has "checked the propagation of the Teutonic stock" (1912 [2009]: 278). Hence, thanksgiving should be offered to Arminius, who crushed the Roman legions of Varus in the Teutoburg Forest in 9 CE; otherwise, the Teutons would have been Latinized vassals of Rome. Rauschenbusch goes on to warn of the danger of this Teutonic blood mixing with French, Slav, "Negro," and, of course, Spanish blood. "Can the racial characteristic of the Teutons hold their predominance against this blending of stock?" he asks (1902 [1989]: 4). His views of Teutonic superiority are unmistakable in the 1902 commencement address, where he celebrates the fact that the Indian fighter, General Custer of Little Big Horn fame (or notoriety), was of German Teutonic stock, "a gallant yellow haired soldier [who] was a grandson of a Hessian officer Kuster, who settled in Pennsylvania" (10–11). While more could be said concerning Rauschenbusch's so-called Teutonic superiority, for purposes of this chapter, we will move toward his ethical thought and its complicity with empire.

Rauschenbusch believed "that the first and the most essential dogma of the Christian faith" was "the Reign of God," first voiced by Jesus in his "parables and prophecies." When "the Reign of God" was ignored, the social ideal of Christendom that existed, "pure and unperverted . . . in the heart of Jesus Christ" was forsaken (1912 [2009]: 49). To remedy this loss, Rauschenbusch proposes establishing the kingdom of God on earth, as it is in heaven—a reign concerned with the core teachings of Jesus, specifically justice, righteousness, social equality, and especially democracy. This, for him, was the doctrine of the social gospel (19). But as Rauschenbusch concentrated on creating a more just and humane Christian social order by impacting the prevailing laws and institutions, that order was, nevertheless, one that continued to see Teutonic-based societies as superior and therefore worth preserving and emulating. He attempted to connect God with the prevailing democratic consciousness of the day in which he was embedded. For Rauschenbusch, the society that was saved was the one, like the U.S., rooted in a democratic order. It is because of this democracy, as Rauschenbusch succinctly put it, that "Jesus is on the side of America" (1911: 106). But while Rauschenbusch saw himself living in a democracy, he failed to make the connection between when he was writing and the consequences of the emerging U.S. Empire for the colonized.

Before the start of the twentieth century, a group of political leaders would socialize at the Metropolitan Club in Washington, D.C., to discuss how the U.S. could become a first-rate nation while saddled with a second-rate military power. Those participating in this discourse included then assistant secretary of the navy Theodore Roosevelt, Admiral George Dewey, Senator Henry Cabot Lodge, and Captain Alfred Thayer Mahan (the most influential writer of his day). They jealously saw European powers carving up the world for colonial exploit and believed that for the United States to be great it must enter the race of conquering foreign lands. Rauschenbusch provided the religious face of colonial exploit by calling for the "moral conquest" of "backward people": "Today the leaders of the missionary movement are teaching a statesmanlike conception of the destiny of Christianity as the spiritual leaven of the East and the common basis of a world-wide Christian civilization. On the foreign field the Christian Church is not yet a conservative force, but a power of moral conquest. There it really embodies the finest spiritual purposes of the Christian nation in the effort to uplift the entire life of the backward people" (1912 [2009]: 18). While those at the Metropolitan Club envisioned the political civilization of the world's natives, Rauschenbusch envisioned their Christianization.

Rauschenbusch, as Stanley Hauerwas correctly points out, was quite militaristic, enthusiastically supporting the Spanish-American War (2000: 85).[2] We can detect Rauschenbusch's hawkish leanings in a jingoistic 1898 Thanksgiving sermon he gave titled *The Present and the Future*, in which he stated, "[The Spanish-American War] is a war for which we give thanks." Reflecting on the war's completion, he goes on to say,

> There is in the heart of our people a deep sense of destiny, of a mission laid upon us by the Ruler of history. . . . [God] has made clear his will by the irrepressible force of events. We shall have to accept and obey. . . . If we rejoice at all in our new imperial domain, we rejoice with fear and trembling. . . . As a nation we must learn to walk by faith and not by sight. And if we have needed the help and light of God in the past, how much more will we need him in the future. (1898 [2009]: 50–51)

This "deep sense of destiny, of a mission," a Manifest Destiny if you will, included the annexation of the spoils of war. And while this "sense of a mission" may have been, in the mind of Rauschenbusch, inspired by the Ruler of history, for those forced to experience the consequences of this missionizing, it was perceived as more satanic than divine.

The war Rauschenbusch supported signified the United States' entry into imperialism (a Protestant imperialism) through the subjugation of foreign people (mainly Roman Catholics), a venture that led to numerous atrocities on the newly possessed islands of Cuba, Puerto Rico, Guam, and the Philippines. Some of the most disturbing acts proceeding from the Spanish-American War occurred on March 7, 1906, when U.S. troops under the command of Major General Leonard Wood massacred as many as 1,000 Filipino Muslims, known as Moros, who were taking refuge at Bud Dajo, a volcanic crater on the island of Jolo in the southern Philippines. Rauschenbusch wrote his classic text, *Christianity and the Social Crisis*, the text that made him famous, at the same time that Filipinos were being massacred by the U.S. imperial armies, publishing the text the very next year, 1907. Apparently, the social crisis of imperialism, the massacre of colonial subjects, and the U.S.' turn from republic to empire are never mentioned in his assessment as to what exactly is the social crisis. While it is not my intention to fault Rauschenbusch for what he failed to say, I do plan to hold him accountable for what he does say, specifically his support for a war that led to these atrocities, and how his words can be perceived as providing justification for the atrocities unfolding in his time. For Hispanic scholars, the social context from which a text arises is as important in the analysis as the text itself.

What Rauschenbusch mentions is disturbing and insensitive, considering the events reported in the nation's daily papers as he wrote his book. He refers to the biblical massacre of the dynasty of Omri of the Northern Kingdom by stating, "[it was] a massacre so fearful that it staggered even the Oriental political conscience" (1907 [1991]: 9). Apparently, even though the "Orientals"[3] were accustomed to massacres, this particular biblical occurrence bothered even them. Yet ironically, Rauschenbusch was silent concerning the massacres in which U.S. troops were engaged. It seems they were not sufficient to stagger his "Occidental" sensibilities.

Rauschenbusch appears to justify such massacres as necessary for civilizing and Christianizing the natives. U.S. conquest of the Philippines is justifiable, regardless of the bloodshed, because public Christian schools are being established.

> When we annexed the Philippines, and our astonished American conscience inquired how we could create foreign dependencies and subject peoples by conquest and purchase like any other bloody tyrant, we hugged the consolation that at any rate the school would follow the flag. In sizing up the future for our Filipino brothers, the commercial corporation was our biggest anxiety, the public school our best justification. The school is Christian; the corporation—not yet. (1912 [2009]: 146)

Justification for colonialism can be found, for Rauschenbusch, in the biblical text. He considers it to have been the destiny of the great power of Assyria to "grind up tribal nationalities of the ancient Orient. . . . [Because] we can see now that the process was inevitable and necessary for the development of a wider and higher civilization, but for those who got between the millstones, it was terror and agony" (1907 [1991]: 24). This quote is more chilling when we consider the "Orientals" of his time being ground up at Bud Dajo.[4]

For Rauschenbusch, empire is an important arsenal in the hands of God. He writes,

> [St.] Paul certainly did not regard the Empire as Satanic in character, but as a divine instrument of order and justice, a power holding the anti-Christian malignity in check. . . . Up to that time [Nero's early years] the persecution of the Christians had all proceeded from the hatred of the Jews, and the strong arm of the Roman government had often served to protect the Christians from the influential malice of the Jews. (1907 [1991]: 110)

Empire, in other words, protects Christians from the Jews of old, or the Filipino Muslims of Rauschenbusch's time, or even the "radical" Muslims of today. But more than protect, it is the means by which the world is saved. Whenever the state or empire was Christianized, Rauschenbusch would argue, "the idea that society and the State were ruled by demons and were anti-Christian in their character, was abandoned" (1907 [1991]: 170). Sounding almost like a present-day neoconservative Christian, Rauschenbusch goes on:

> [Christian thinkers have] often dwelt on the fact that Christianity had been born simultaneously with the Empire under Augustus. The universal State and the universal religion were twins by birth. They ought, therefore, to be in helpful relations to each other in accordance with the manifest purpose of God. . . . [T]he Church could be the best ally of the State in creating civil peace, because Christians had the highest morality, and because they alone had power over the demons who menaced the security of the Empire. As the soul holds the body together, so Christians hold the world together. (114–15)

Rauschenbusch does condemn colonialism, specifically Belgium's ventures in the Congo, for its "militant capitalism," which is responsible for "rotting human lives" (270). He is correct in condemning empires of the past—for example, the Roman Empire—for failing to distribute wealth in a just manner, and he is right to warn of the danger in which the U.S. will put itself if it emulates Rome (281–86).[5]

Still, for Rauschenbusch, the problem is not with the empire per se, but with the personal piety of Christians within the empire. For Rauschenbusch, as Stanley Hauerwas points out, the saving of the nation (empire?) is inseparable from the saving of the church (2000: 82). Rauschenbusch concludes by connecting the early Christian church with the imperialist project upon which the U.S. has embarked in his time, thus defending and glorifying the emerging U.S. Empire while ignoring the atrocities committed to make empire a reality.

> Today [1907] we have a similar process of international amalgamation very similar to that of the early Christian centuries. At that time a new and common civilization was growing up around the Mediterranean Sea; today it is growing up around all the oceans. It is significant that the prophets of the modern social movement are also the prophets of a new internationalism, which aims to supplant the narrow patriotisms and interests of a by-gone stage of human development by the wider enthusiasms and outlooks of a vaster human brotherhood. There is a profound similarity between the consciousness and the aims of early Christianity and of modern social thought, wherever it has ethical and religious impetus in it. (1907 [1991]: 115–16)

For Rauschenbusch, the world is to be redeemed by a United States that is central to God's plan. This position is disturbing, especially when we consider who is influencing his thoughts. Rauschenbusch honors men like Josiah Strong (1912 [2009]: 9), whose Manifest Destiny vision saw God "training the Anglo-Saxon race" to extend its power "upon Mexico, down upon Central and South America, out upon the islands of the sea, over upon Africa and beyond." This "competition of races" would conclude with the "survival of the fittest" (Smith, 1963: 85–87). If this is the case, then the victory of the Spanish-American War, for Rauschenbusch, is evidence of a national religious energy coming out of the depths of God (1914: 732–33). God is calling U.S. churches to fulfill their historical destiny. This imperial calling is not one that Americans seek, but one that they must, out of obedience, accept as fulfilling their duty in accordance with the divine will. Rauschenbusch captures this jingoistic sentiment in an 1881 poem he wrote on July 4th titled "My Country."

Safe while we trust in God
Bow to His mighty Rod
. . .
Raise high the beacon-light,
Pierce through the world's black night
Show her the noble sight of liberty. (1881 [2009]: 26)

REINHOLD NIEBUHR

The social optimism of the turn of the twentieth century advocated by Rauschenbusch's social gospel gave way to the Christian realism of ethicists like Reinhold Niebuhr—a realism that seriously considered human opposition to God due to the "sin of pride" (1941: 186–203). While ethical realism can be applauded for its incorporation of analytical tools to discern reality, still, in spite of Niebuhr's claim that he based his ethical thoughts on realism, it remains an excellent example of idealistic ethics. Why? Because his ethics lacks the multiple consciousnesses required to perceive what constitutes realism, and how that reality operates to preserve and maintain the prideful status quo designed to privilege one group at the expense of others.

Still, Hispanic ethicists, along with other proponents of liberationist ethics, can find agreement with a Niebuhrian realism that recognizes that any claim concerning justice is both contextual and historical. This is a realism that understands that power lies with those who are economically privileged, occupying leading roles within the dominant social structure, which enables them to shape and form a reality undergirded by their views and intellectual positions justifying their privilege and power. Unfortunately, the Niebuhrian approach to social conflict fails to make any preferential option for the side that is marginalized. Niebuhr's attempt at some objective power diplomacy within a democratic system creates a type of neutrality unable to assess the depth of marginalization. Operating solely from a white middle-class consciousness, Niebuhr need not understand what routinely happens in marginalized communities. He can create ethical paradigms without having to comprehend what it means to be of color, specifically Latino/a, in America. Stereotypes soon fill in the gaps for him. Lacking the epistemological privilege of those forced to live and operate in the world dominated by his race and class, or of those living in the disenfranchised world located at his underside, prevents his ethics from fully grasping the reality of the prevailing social structures.

Ironically, Niebuhr, a member of the Socialist Party, expressed a more socialist-based ethics in his early writings (1930s and 1940s) as he railed against "immoral society," no doubt influenced by the thirteen years he spent ministering to dehumanized car assembly-line workers in Detroit. But in his later writing (1950s and 1960s), he became an apologist for the so-called free world, advocating for a pragmatic realism based on cold-war conservatism that tolerated injustices and justified the U.S. role as empire. By the conclusion of the Second World War, Niebuhr believed the U.S. held a moral responsibility to assume the role of world leadership over and against a Communism that was "a vivid object lesson in the monstrous consequences of moral complacency about the relation of dubious means to supposedly good ends" (1952: 5). This leadership role that the Anglo-Saxon race was to play in the world was God ordained (1943: 2), their manifest destiny if you will. But to assume that Niebuhr arrived at this view only after the carnage of the Second World War and the unstable world order that preceded the conclusion of the war masks how he also advocated U.S. imperialism before the war. When considering the alternatives to Nazism, Niebuhr believed Anglo-Saxon imperialism was the best possible option within a "realistic imperialistic" world order (1942: 3–6).

Although conscious that the U.S. might become too imperialistic, Niebuhr feared more the global anarchy emerging in the wake of the Second World War. In spite of the possible downsides to empire, he called the U.S. to "responsible" imperialism. For U.S.-assumed global leadership to be effective, order within society and in the global arena is needed, even when order creates certain injustices. Ethics, for the U.S., becomes defined as minimizing injustices within a sphere of restraint in the U.S. overreach while avoiding the pitfalls of conducting itself in a prideful manner. Some may see the early Niebuhr as different from the later Niebuhr; nevertheless, it seems that both are rooted in the same anthropology, operating from basic racial and ethnic assumptions that did not change much in his long writing career.

For example, even in his more liberal, progressive, socialist early writings, he defended the racial underpinnings of empire to maintain order. Niebuhr bases his moral reasoning on a Eurocentric, class-defined anthropology that remains disconnected from the life experiences of marginalized communities in the U.S. Although Niebuhr occasionally wrote against America's racism and segregation practices, it never was a major thrust in his work or activism. For him, racism was reduced to a manifestation of the sin of pride. "All human groups are essentially proud and find that pride very convenient because it seems to justify their special privileges and to explain the sad state of the underprivileged. It is this combination of selfishness and pride which makes the problems of group relationships so difficult" (1928: 1046). For Niebuhr, humanity is beset by the selfishness of hubris. But as Susan Thistlethwaite reminds us, "Valerie Saiving and then Judith Plaskow have held that 'sin for woman' is better described as the failure to be a self" (2003: 9).[6] I would add that "sin for Hispanics" is similar. Nevertheless, Niebuhr insists that "minorities have developed a pride of their own to compensate for their unconscious inferiority complex" (1928: 1046). From this perspective, he can paternalistically advise African Americans in their struggle for civil rights. But such advice, as offered by Niebuhr, is couched in an understanding of the black's placement at a lower evolutionary stage. In calling for boycotts against stores and banks that discriminate against African Americans, Niebuhr advises that "He [the African American] would need only to fuse the aggressiveness of the new and young Negro with the patience and forbearance of the old Negro, to rob the former of its vindictiveness and the latter of its lethargy" (1932: 254). For Niebuhr, the Negro's patience and forbearance are not due to religious virtue, but rather racial weakness (1932: 268).

Although Niebuhr probably said more about racial inequality than any other Euroamerican ethicist of his time, his pronouncements on the subject remain troublesome. He seems more focused on the disruptive impact that civil rights could have on Southern culture than on the injustices faced by blacks. He advises African Americans not to make too many demands too quickly. Civil rights for blacks are good and fine, as long as those rights do not disrupt order (here read as white privilege). Ethicist Traci West reminds us, "unfortunately Niebuhr did not similarly propose that whites like himself should engage in these tactics in order to challenge racial discrimination at stores and banks that *they* used" (2006: 13; emphasis in original). It should not be surprising, as West points out, that during the 1950s move toward desegregation, Niebuhr expresses sympathy for those "anxious parents" who oppose school desegregation because of "the cultural differences" of the two races. Niebuhr can hope that someday "the Negro people will have the same advantages as our children" (15), but not at the price of social order. Order is to be pursued, even at the price of certain inequalities—a proposition incongruent with any marginalized community committed to justice. When writing during his more progressive younger years, Niebuhr made room for certain inequalities, regarding them as necessary for the proper functioning of society: "No complex society will be able to dispense with certain inequalities of privilege. Some of them are necessary for the proper performance of certain social functions; and others (though this is not so certain) may be needed to prompt energy and diligence in the performance of important functions" (1932: 128). Niebuhr relates ethical principles like justice, liberty, and social order to the Christian concept of love. Although these ethical principles are not necessarily in conflict with each other, Niebuhr believes they should be prioritized. The global disarray following the Second World War and the need for a stable world order in a nuclear age led Niebuhr to make a preferential option for order, even at the cost of certain inequalities.

Niebuhr is not the only Eurocentric ethicist who is willing to accept inequalities for the good of society. Other ethicists, from his era to today, have also strengthened the empire's hold by advocating order. Paul Ramsey, for example, while calling for equitable race relations, critiqued lunch counter sit-ins conducted by blacks as an improper social Christian action because it disrupted society's law and order (1961: 48–49). For John Rawls, the establishment of justice was to be encouraged as long as it remained constrained within the limits of a well-ordered society (1971: 453–57). And even James Gustafson was comfortable with the pursuit of justice as long as it did not upset "a necessary equilibrium in society" (1975: 119–20). The ethics of the majority of Euroamerican ethicists exists to preserve the established order, not just of their society and their place within that society, but, I would argue, of the empire as well, and the U.S. Empire's place in the world. Whenever ethics is reduced to maintaining law and order, justice is sacrificed on the altar of Niebuhr's pragmatism.

The cost of Niebuhr's realism to the Hispanic community, paid in underdevelopment and minimal resources, is too high. The pragmatism expressed by such Euroamerican idealistic ethicists undermines any movements toward liberation through the establishment of justice by reinforcing the prevailing power structures grounded in the empire. For the liberationist, Euroamerican realism is the problem. In the name of realism, ethics fails to challenge the status quo, forcing liberationist ethicist José Míguez Bonino to point out,

> The true question is not "What degree of justice (liberation of the poor) is compatible with the maintenance of the existing order?" but "what kind of order, which order is compatible with the exercise of justice (the right of the poor)?" Here alone do we find an adequate point of departure for the theological determination of priorities. The fix point is "justice, the rights of the poor." . . . Justice is the foundation of order. (1983: 86)

Niebuhr's commitment to Christian realism leads him, and many present-day Euroamerican ethicists, to the conclusion that the ideal of love as the basis for public action is simply impractical, for it is unable to deal with the complexities of modern life. Based on the forced dualism of Augustine's "two cities," the thirteenth-century canonists' "two luminaries," and/or Martin Luther's "two kingdoms," a dichotomy is constructed between the "private" and "public," where the former places the individual under the dictates of God while the latter creates a rationale that justifies whatever powers and principalities are in place. Nations, multinational corporations, and other collective entities (e.g., empire), say these ethicists, are, unlike humans, simply incapable of moral behavior, a proposition found intolerable by those Hispanics forced to exist on the underside of such entities. Niebuhr's realism, based on this radical dualism, liberates political powers from the demands of the gospel message. In the name of realism, oppressive structures become a necessity of law and order.

By the 1950s, Niebuhr's realism becomes an apologetics for U.S. global dominance. Toward the end of his teaching career he writes *The Structure of Nations and Empires*. Studying the recurring historical phenomena of the inevitability of empire, he gleans lessons that the U.S. can adopt to fulfill its global hegemonic responsibilities and check what he perceives as the Soviet Union's global aggressiveness. Niebuhr's realistic liberalism in his later writings contains the same racist assumptions of his earlier writings. These racial assumptions take on global proportions when he concludes in *The Structure of Nations and Empires* that colonialism is a necessary step toward the development of civilization for those countries that were "on the primitive level of tribal life" or, in the case of China and India, lacking technical means of communication important for community

cohesiveness (1959: 202). Niebuhr believes that the lack of technological advances in Two-Thirds World nations, as well as their lack
of receptivity to democracy, leads to resentment toward the centers
of technical power, resentment that is exploited by the Communist
East (1952: 123–27).

Niebuhr did not see colonialism as a moral evil, but rather as a
moral ambiguity where the "tutelage of colonialism," he maintained,
could benefit humanity (1959: 25). The concept of imperialism
could be neutral, and in some cases, a positive force for the human
condition. He felt that empire, in and of itself, was not an immoral
form of dominion, for those who govern by it could serve as trust-
ees for civilization and "bestow a value of universal validity" (203).
Unlike empires of old that may have been more harmful than beneficial, the U.S. empire of Niebuhr's time was merely a "servant to
the universal community" (22).

But the concept of the U.S. as servant-leader within an imperial
global order is highly problematic. Under the subsection titled "The
Imperial Responsibility," Niebuhr writes,

> [Our anti-imperialism] does make for a certain hesitancy in
> exercising the responsibility of our imperial power, since we
> fear that we violate the cardinal principle of liberalism, the "self-
> determination of nations." We cannot afford such hesitancy, even
> in a world in which the weak nations are as preoccupied with anti-
> imperialistic slogans as we are. If social conditions of our client
> nations—whether in South Vietnam, South Korea, or possibly,
> Saudi Arabia—are the kind which invite Communist infiltra-
> tion, we must exercise the responsibilities of our power to correct
> them, even if such a policy can be effective only if the power
> is exercised with a minimal affront to the dignity of sovereign
> nations. (1962b: 158)

In Niebuhr's mind, the U.S., while not seeking it, became the most
powerful nation in human history because of its moral superiority.
The U.S.' "moral advantage lies in the fact that [it] does not have
a strong lust for power which always accompanies its possession"
(1952: 38). And although he was quick to point out the shortcomings and sins of a morally superior United States, specifically its
pride and egotism, he still finds it superior to all other nations and
systems of governance, most of which, by comparison, have greater
shortcomings and sins.

In his call for imperialistic intervention to counter Communism's "absurd religio-political creed" (1962a: 15), Niebuhr remains unconscious of his own neoliberal infiltration. Perceiving the dangers the Soviet Communist threat poses, he is oblivious to the inhumane and uncivilized threat of savage capitalism as unleashed by multinational corporations. It is for this reason that Niebuhrian realism must be rejected, for it is, and continues to be, an ethical paradigm constructed with the explicit goal of making a preferential option for the political and economic interest of the U.S. Empire, and, as such, it is by definition against the interests of U.S. Latina/os and their extended families still living in their nations of origin.

By the early sixties, Niebuhr's belief that Two-Thirds World countries can provide the U.S. the opportunity to extend its "tutelage" upon them evolves into an imperialist stance that maintains social order even if the country in question is operated through a brutal military dictatorship. He wrote, "Dangerous as [military dictatorships] are, they are at least reversible and Communist dictatorship, supported by a religio-political dogma, is irreversible" (1961: 12). Niebuhr's unapologetic advocacy of imperialism in his ethics may be justifiable in his mind as a pragmatic response to the international realities that call for checking "god-less" communism; but for those of us who originated in those military dictatorships and experienced the poverty, terror, disappearance, and death endemic to U.S.-sponsored national-security states, Niebuhr's ethics concerning the U.S. Empire can only be interpreted as satanic.

Missing from Niebuhr's analysis is how he, and other ethicists like him, directly benefit from their complicity with an empire that provides them with a disproportionate standard of living due to the dominant cultures' acquisition of cheap labor, raw material, and potential markets for dumping surplus finished products, regardless of all the benefits Niebuhr seems to think the oppressed gain from their subservient relationship with the empire. The real question Niebuhr thinks needs answering is how the U.S. Empire that emerged after the Second World War can responsibly assume and use its newfound role as a superpower for good (1959: 15). But central to Niebuhr's praise for empire is the same racist presupposition that appeared in his earlier writings, namely, that empires are run by those who think themselves superior. He writes, "Power need not be expressed in military terms. . . . The desire to expand the superior culture is one of the motives of imperial expansion" (66). And this is the crux of why his ethics is unacceptable to the Hispanic community.

What makes Niebuhr's ethics incongruent with the Hispanic hope for liberative ethics is how Niebuhr (re)members history. When describing the U.S. Empire, in contrast with the Soviet Empire, Niebuhr claims that the U.S. has an "anti-imperial animus and [a] continental expanse . . . [that] made imperial ventures unnecessary" (1959: 12). Niebuhr would be willing to forget what Latina/os cannot. U.S. imperial lust for cheap labor and raw material has led to twenty-one military incursions and twenty-six covert operations in Central American and Caribbean nations during the twentieth century. Imperial ventures, euphemistically called "gun-boat diplomacy," have always been the norm perpetrated against our nations of origin; yet, in Niebuhr's mind, they are conveniently forgotten.[7]

STANLEY HAUERWAS

Let us now turn our attention to the last ethicist we will consider from the twentieth century, Stanley Hauerwas. He is credited with developing a narrative theology and is a pioneer in the recovery of virtue within the theological ethics discourse. Additionally, he has renewed the centrality of ecclesiology and has been consistent in his critique of political liberalism[8] as a public theologian. Although his critique of the Enlightenment Project and liberal individualism and his emphasis on community are refreshing and should be applauded, his lack of a prophetic ethics is troublesome.

My main concern is that Hauerwas, while recognizing the importance of justice, fails to make this the underlying characteristic of the kingdom of God. He writes, "the current emphasis on justice and rights as the primary norms guiding the social witness of Christians is in fact a mistake" (1991: 45). Elsewhere he writes, "Christian social ethics is not first of all principles or policies for social action, but rather the story of God's calling of Israel and the life of Jesus" (1985: 181–82). The primary task of the church "is not to *make* the world the kingdom, but to be faithful to the kingdom by showing to the world what it means to be a community of peace" (1983: 103). Not surprisingly, then, in attempting to recover virtue ethics, Hauerwas fails to advocate praxis and shows antipathy toward establishing justice-based principles upon which to foster praxis. For Hauerwas, any attempt to establish social justice is more a response to the Enlightenment project than it is to the gospel. For

Christians to participate in such justice-based praxis is to become complicit with the hegemonic liberalism of the world (1997: 190–91, 195). Thus, to be a moral agent is more a process of learning how to see reality through a Eurocentric Christian lens than it is a process of enunciating praxes that challenge, subvert, or undermine the oppressive structures reinforced in society by that way of seeing. In short, the Christian must remain aloof to "political change and justice," as well as "progressive forces" (1985: 185). The social ethics advocated by Hauerwas, in the final analysis, is but a gesture (186). Although gestures may be meaningful for the privileged, they are, unfortunately, meaningless for those relegated to hunger, thirst, nakedness, alienation, incarceration, or illness.

In *Vision and Virtue* Hauerwas proposes that ethics is the conceptual discipline that analyzes and imaginatively tests the images most appropriate to score the Christian life. While he does not deny the importance of action, living a moral life becomes for him a form of aesthetics concerned with learning how to articulate one's moral visions and notions, or as Hauerwas would say,

> The ethical problem reflects a classical priority in seeking to know the truth rather than to choose or will the good. . . . Such truthful vision, however does not come without discipline. . . . [But s]uch discipline is not a code of conduct but rather the willingness to stand and accept the reality of the other without neurotic self-regard or the comfort of convention. (1974: 2)

Theological ethics for Hauerwas is orthodoxy; it proceeds from the doctrine of the Christian faith. Orthodoxy leads to how the church thinks about, formulates, and/or engages in orthopraxis, the reversal of the liberationist formula that insists theological and ethical reflections proceed from praxis—the doing of ethics. As he points out, "The first task of Christian social ethics, therefore, is not to make the 'world' better or more just, but to help Christian people form their community consistent with their conviction that the story of Christ is a truthful account of our existence" (1981: 112). He confuses an unapologetic conviction of the truth of the Christian narrative with a Eurocentric interpretation of what that truth might be, thereby converting his truth claims into a facade masking a power that reinforces Eurocentric Christian dominance in the discourse as well as the culture. The community becomes the place where "praxis," understood as behaviors or personal piety that emulates the kingdom of God, takes place. Dismantling oppressive societal structures is not as important as developing a Christian character. Missing is a prophetic call that grounds ethical thought in the actual dismantlement of oppressive structures apart from the church community.

For Hauerwas, "Christian ethics is best understood as an ethics of character" (1975: vii). Nevertheless, for the U.S. marginalized, Christian ethics is best understood as an ethics of societal change! Simply stated, there can exist no significant ethics without an emphasis on praxis. Although it is noble to envision how character ought to be seen and intended, and how it might influence behavior that might bring about change, it is only through praxis geared at dismantling the power and privilege bestowed upon Euroamericans and their churches that character develops. For what good is a virtuous character if oppressive structures remain? Just as faith without works is dead (James 2:20), so too are right virtues without right praxis meaningless.

Hauerwas insists that a moral agent's self-understanding of his or her actions (as opposed to how others may interpret those actions) is the foundation of his or her morality. Specifically, that foundation is "what kind of agents they think themselves to be in doing what they do" (1977: 649). The danger to Hispanics in such a moral vision is that it provides a virtuous way of conduct that ignores the "virtuous" complicity with the structures of empire that cause oppression. This complicity is further masked through Hauerwas' understanding of ecclesiology. He advises that "the church and Christians must be uninvolved in the polity of our society and involved in the polity that is the church" (1981: 74). Rather than making a preferential option for the marginalized, as most liberationists do, Hauerwas makes a preferential option for the church—specifically, the U.S. church, which cannot avoid its complicity with empire, even though Hauerwas may rail against empire.

As Hauerwas often states, "the church does not have a social ethic; the church is a social ethic" (1983: 99). When he calls the church "to be the church," Hauerwas intends for the church to serve the world, which desperately needs to hear the "truth" of the Christian narrative (2004: 231). But how can Latina/os trust a church, or the social ethics advocated by a church, that historically has been Eurocentric, anti-Semitic, racist, sexist, and colonialist, and in many cases continues to be so?[9] If, as Hauerwas claims, "the primary social task of the church is to be itself" (1981: 10), then all people of color need to be *very* concerned, for this is a church whose ethics has historically accommodated and justified every form of human exploitation—from massacres to war, from slavery to colonialism. Just as Hauerwas assumed that the oppression at the church he attended while growing up in segregated Texas was "normal," he continues to fail to recognize how oppression for Hispanics is normalized today by his Euroamerican churches (1997: 225). Centuries of white supremacy cannot be washed away simply because Hauerwas envisions what the church of Christ ought to be. Regardless of how progressive Hauerwas' vision of the church may be, it offers little or no hope for the salvation of Latina/os because he has failed to deconstruct the power dynamics embedded in the type of church attended by Euroamericans of relative privilege like him. When Hauerwas insists that "there is no ideal church, no mystically existing church more real than the concrete church of parking lots and potluck dinners" (1983: 107), he betrays how embedded he is in his white middle-class understanding of church. The storefront or home church of many Hispanics has no parking lot and can seldom afford potluck dinners. For many Latino/as, the church is the concreteness of fried baloney sandwiches. For Hauerwas, the proper response to world hunger and neighborhood poverty is to reclaim the significance of the trivial—to enjoy a walk, to read novels, play sports, or worship God. To indulge in the trivial affirms God's patience (1988: 256–57). But claiming God's patience in the face of the hunger of others is definitely a middle-class privilege. It is obvious that his church is not the church of those forced to eat fried baloney; those working multiple jobs to avoid hunger have no time to take a walk, read novels, or play sports. And I can assure you, they worship God very differently. Saving lemurs, as an example of a trivial act suggested by Hauerwas, may be a way peace becomes concretely embodied in Euroamericans lives (1988: 260), but it is not how it is embodied in the lives of those who exist on their underside, who are more concerned with saving their families and themselves. Liturgy may be an effective social action for Hauerwas (1985: 187), but dispossessed Hispanics need something more than just liturgy.

Even though Hauerwas admits that he has "no idea how deeply the habits of racism are written into [his] life;" he still refuses to use the voices of the marginalized to inform his ethical analysis. "Still, for me," Hauerwas writes,

[T]o "use" Martin Luther King Jr., and the church that made him possible, to advance my understanding of "Christian ethics" seems wrong. That is not my story, though I pray that God will make that story my story, for I hope to enjoy the fellowship of the communion of the saints. Yet that is an eschatological hope, which, as much as one desires it, cannot be forced. (1997: 225–26)

Because, as Hauerwas acknowledges, he is a "white southerner from the lower-middle classes who grew up embedded in the practices of segregation" (225), Martin Luther King Jr.'s story *is* Hauerwas' story. And because it is, he need not wait for the eschaton to enjoy the fellowship of the communion of saints. Praxis can make such communion possible in the here-and-now. In fact, the lack of such communion serves as testimony that although the segregated church Hauerwas privileges may consist of a gathering of people of similar cultural and socioreligious backgrounds, it is no church, it is no body of Christ consisting of diverse parts.

Ethicists like Hauerwas who are not directly impacted by oppressive structures, nor are interested in solidarity with the dispossessed, have the luxury of pontificating morality. His myopia and/or refusal to consider the social location of the oppressed undermines his entire ethical structure, as can be illustrated in his proposition that a narrative ethics based on Jesus teaches him to be a pacifist. Although he may be advocating pacifism, his dismissal of marginalized voices makes him and his ethics complicit with an institutional violence that, like war, is also responsible for death. Jesus may have taught Hauerwas not to kill, but Hauerwas failed to learn from Jesus that death does not solely come from the barrel of a gun. Death is also caused by economic, social, and political structures, and Hauerwas' refusal to consider seriously the plight of the disenfranchised negates his advocacy for pacifism. It also negates the Jesus narrative he holds supreme by not centering it on the "doing to the very least of these."

In spite of Hauerwas' attempted engagement with liberative ethics or theology, we should not be surprised when he dismisses Gustavo Gutiérrez's work on liberation theology as "profoundly anti-Christian," an inadequate theological and sociological expression of liberal theology (1986: 69).[10] More disturbing is his argument against the hope of salvation from oppression by reminding the marginalized that salvation is, in fact, "a life that freely suffers, that freely serves, because such suffering and service is the hallmark of the Kingdom established by Jesus" (69–70). Hispanics should always be concerned when Euroamerican ethicists tell them why their suffering, caused by Euroamericans in the first place, makes them better saved Christians! It is obvious to those excluded from the churches of the dominant culture that the church of which Hauerwas writes is not their church. Because Christian churches continue to be segregated in terms of race, ethnicity, and class, the Eurocentric church Hauerwas seems to privilege remains embedded within the power structures of empire so that he need not freely suffer—only abstractly; nevertheless, those same structures that protect him from such suffering are paid for with the actual suffering and death of Hispanics and other communities of color.[11] Since the normative U.S. church is white and middle class, a type of sectarian ecclesiology is created, as James Gustafson points out, to which Hauerwas can retreat (1985: 83–94). Unfortunately, this retreat leads to a civil irresponsibility, which can be illustrated by the present immigration debate.

For purposes of discussion, let us examine one of the virtues Hauerwas privileges, the virtue of hospitality. Although Hauerwas has attempted to distance himself from "virtue ethics," he takes seriously the narratively mandated virtue of hospitality. For him, "the truthfulness of Christian conviction resides in [that truth's] power to form a people sufficient to acknowledge the divided character of the world and thus necessarily be ready to offer hospitality to the stranger" (1981: 93). Nevertheless, he fails to articulate how to make this hospitality a reality within the community. For Hauerwas, the truthfulness of hospitality remains an eschatological reality. Although hoped for—in a limited way—within the church, hospitality is a process of becoming that will find its full completion in the eschatological future.

The shortcomings of Hauerwas' "virtue of hospitality" are twofold. First, one would assume that a praxis of hospitality that Hauerwas could advocate is for churches to participate in the sanctuary movement (either the 1980s version or the present day New Sanctuary Movement). Hauerwas may participate in moral public discourse, but he remains silent on advocating praxis (even civil disobedience) as the means by which the church becomes the church. We can applaud him for advocating a virtue of hospitality, but we must remain critical of a pursuit of this virtue that neither leads to direct action nor develops suggestions as to what policies the U.S.

should follow concerning the issue of undocumented immigration. The virtue of hospitality absent praxis may be beneficial to those churchgoers privileged with residency, but it remains life threatening to the undocumented congregant. And second, to practice the virtue of hospitality assumes the "house" belongs to the one practicing this virtue, who is sharing her or his resources with the Other, who has no claim to the possession. Thus the complexity caused by the consequences of empire is missed. For example, consider Mexican undocumented aliens. Their "house" was stolen from them when the U.S. invaded Mexico in 1845 and through superior military might appropriated what is now called the southwestern United States. Rather than speaking about the virtue of hospitality, it would historically be more accurate to speak about the responsibility of restitution.

Here then is how Hauerwas' tendency toward abstraction, where his vision supersedes contextualized praxis, reinforces the Eurocentric ability to control the discourse, and thus reinforces empire. By separating his vision of what the virtue of hospitality is from the everyday experience of the Hispanic undocumented in need of the praxis of hospitality, he sets up an intellectual world where his propositions can never be validated. Focusing on how the church is to *be* rather than how it is to *have* a social ethics moves the discourse to the abstract. Such abstract discussions have little or no value to those whose very survival depends on the church *doing* a social ethics—though in the minds of those comfortable with such abstraction his pronouncements on ethics are therefore legitimized even if they fail to provide any liberative praxis for those residing on the underside of Euroamerican culture. I find more in common with Muslims, Hindus, or Jews who are faithful to their sacred texts' call for justice than I do with Hauerwas' brand of Christianity, which argues "why justice is a bad idea for Christians" (1991: 45–68).[12] Hauerwas' ethical pronouncements, along with other Eurocentric ethical paradigms that focus on the abstract rather than contextualized praxis, can have no standing within the Latina/o community specifically, because such praxis is too anemic. Ironically, the church Hauerwas tends to privilege ceases to be the church because it lacks the types of praxis consistently called for by God as recorded within the biblical narrative. For only through Christian praxis is the Christian church established. Any church lacking praxis is not a Christian church, but a collective of individuals with common traits, no different than an exclusive country club.

A WORD ON VIRTUE

Among Eurocentric Christian ethicists, much emphasis is given to areteological ethics, which centers on living a life of virtues based on the presupposition that good actions flow from good character. Virtue, according to Robin Lovin, is cultivated when a pattern of behavior learned through practice becomes a way individuals tend to act. Virtue becomes a habit continuously and instinctively performed without much contemplation. From this virtuous character, ethics is produced. Still, Hispanics have lived a history, and continue to live a life, of suffering, oppression, and death by social structures created by and for the privilege of good Christians with virtuous characters. Not surprisingly, Hispanics feel a certain apprehension when virtue ethics is advocated.

While Lovin is conscious that at times virtue can be limited to a particular culture or social location, he still insists that it is plausible to recognize a few universal moral rules—virtues that every single culture would agree are "just right" (2000: 63–67). Grounding ethics on individualist contemplation is probably best articulated by Immanuel Kant. But contrary to Kant's presupposition that ethics are to be relegated to the private sphere (the human's a priori moral sense upon which the "categorical imperative"[13] is based), all ethics are communal with social consequences. For virtue ethicists, personal piety or the demonstration of virtues is equated with ethics; yet, for Hispanics, ethics can never be reduced to individual traits, for no matter how personal we wish to make ethics, it always has a collective dimension. Ignoring or minimizing this dimension is the root of all injustices. Although personal piety and virtuous living are desirable qualities for Hispanics, they can never be the totality of ethics. While the state of individualistic being constitutes the bases for most Eurocentric ethical paradigms, for Latino/as (and most U.S. communities of color), communal doing is the cornerstone upon which they begin to do praxis, that is, begin to do ethics.

Even though virtue ethicists may recognize that complicity with the dominant culture might exist, they underestimate the extent of that complicity. Missing is a thorough analysis of how the power relationship existing within society constructs, interprets, and defines what is considered a virtue. Virtues, whether beneficial or detrimental to the disenfranchised communities, are in the final analysis a construct of what the dominant culture deems morally good or evil. By constructing virtues and employing the myth of objectivity, that culture legitimizes and normalizes injustices within society. Should we therefore be surprised that a Eurocentric culture, based on a capitalist economic system whose salient characteristic is hyperindividuality, would label sloth as foundational in defining sin? And that the same culture would therefore deem "the Protestant work ethic" a virtue? To be industrious and not lazy may indeed be good, and thus deserve to be encouraged, but this "virtue" has more to do with the economic good of society than with Christian ethics. And what may be a virtue for the dominant culture can easily be detrimental to oppressed groups. A brief illustration will demonstrate this point. While slave masters during the antebellum period preached against the vice of laziness and for the virtues of hard work, the slave understood that sloth was an act of resistance against the injustices upon which society was based and that he therefore had a moral obligation to do the least amount of work possible as a means of preserving his life and the lives of the rest of the slave community, even at the risk of being stereotyped as lazy.

As desirable as cultivating certain virtues may be, their implementation can at first ignore, and then justify, unjust social structures. For example, the individual may practice the virtue of hospitality, yet be incredulous when confronted with the dominant culture's complicity with the human rights violations occurring along the U.S. southern border, violations targeting brown skin. The culture becomes complicit either by refusing to implement communal praxis to disrupt the status quo or, more likely, through ignorance that any human rights are being violated. Worse than failing to effectively challenge social structures, the practice of virtue by an individual creates a false sense of righteousness. The virtue ethicists might call for reform, but because of the salient individualistic character of virtue ethics, based in part on self-reliance, absent from the discourse is consideration of correcting the unjust distribution of wealth and power. Reform may be called for, but dismantling of the structures responsible for privileging whiteness and economic class is not.

Even when we attempt to base virtues on rights, the rights that receive a preferential option are those that continue to sustain the status of the dominant culture. Not all rights are equal. All may agree that humans have a right to receive a daily sufficient amount of calories to sustain life. Nourishment, especially in the richest country the world has ever known, may be a basic human right;

and yet this right is assaulted by other rights that take precedence. Regardless of hunger, an individual cannot jump a fence to take an apple from a tree, nor even an abandoned apple that fell off a tree and is in the process of rotting on the ground. To jump the fence and trespass on another's land violates property rights. If the violator is arrested, the circumstance of dire hunger and the basic human right to survive are not legal arguments for violating property rights. When it comes to human rights versus property rights, the latter are privileged. The fact that protection of property rights, even in the face of human death, is given a preferential option demonstrates how "rights" language is used to maintain the law and order required for the few to continue enriching themselves in spite of the consequences to disenfranchised communities.

Those seeking to maintain unjust social structures have learned that creating their own "rights" or "virtues" to compete with one of the basic human rights of disenfranchised communities provides them the semblance of a moral argument that perpetuates oppression. For example, the right of indigenous Mexicans and Central Americans to return to their ancestral lands to feed their families, who are economically devastated by unfair trade policies (e.g., NAFTA) designed to benefit the U.S., is countered with moral arguments like (1) the right of Americans to secure their borders, or (2) the virtue of obeying the laws of the land and not "jumping" to the head of the line. One of the consequences of constructing opposing rights or virtues is the worsening of the social and economic predicament of Hispanics.

No one questions that the language of virtues and rights may lead to desirable behavior, or that personal piety is good and should be pursued by all humans. Nevertheless, such language has historically marginalized, and continues to marginalize, the Latina/o community. For this reason, an uncritical adaptation of the virtues and rights of the dominant culture is detrimental to Latino/as specifically, because those virtues and rights are constructed by those who would benefit if all marginalized groups were to adopt their moral standards.

FAILURE OF EUROCENTRIC ETHICS

What Walter Rauschenbusch, Reinhold Niebuhr, and Stanley Hauerwas have in common is that they successfully created paradigms that failed to grasp how empire is fundamentally a Eurocentric problem—a problem that the academic discipline we call "ethics" aids and abets. For the dominant culture to then insist that their ethical analysis and paradigms must become foundational in the Hispanic quest for liberation—*la lucha para la liberación*—is ludicrous. Why? Because the driving force responsible for maintaining a status quo that privileges one group at the expense of people of colors, specifically Hispanics, is a Eurocentric-driven culture—a culture in which Latina/os are the object, the problem, never the subject, the solution. For members of that culture to reconcile the empire that benefits them with their commitment to Christianity requires an abstract ethics that, while distinctly Eurocentric, can be presented as universal. As such, ethics becomes a Eurocentric construct that is part of a larger metanarrative that privileges the vision and virtues of Euroamericans. One cannot serve two masters: God and mammon; in the same way, Latino/as cannot adhere to two ethical paradigms: a liberative ethics seeking justice for Hispanics and a Eurocentric ethics embedded in the empire.

Even so, the ultimate failure of these ethicists, as well as those ethicists or scholars who uncritically subscribe to the dominant culture's worldview, is that they have refused to do a serious power analysis and to locate themselves within the prevailing power structures. Their complicity with empire relieves them, they suppose, of any responsibility for actually establishing a justice that can be liberating for the Hispanic community, or any other marginalized community. Eurocentric ethics is a product of power—power held by those who benefit by making their ethics normative. As such, Eurocentric ethics is not an exercise in establishing justice, but rather a justification for activating power. The Euroamerican ethical discourse becomes a strategy for reconciling some type of moral reasoning with the existing structures, which remain detrimental to Latina/os, without sacrificing the privilege amassed by the prevailing ethics of the dominant culture.

No doubt most ethicists are well-meaning Euroamericans who believe in equality and are vocal in their desire to encourage diversity in the discourse, yet they unconsciously allow the social structures undergirding the academy and guild to discriminate for them. By reducing racism to the bigot, they ignore how Euroamerican scholars who are well versed in race analysis still remain complicit with racist structures that exclude scholars of color. To break away from the prevailing Eurocentric metanarrative, which at times constructs

Hispanics as objects and problems to the dominant culture, but mostly simply ignores them, a counternarrative is required. This false "Hispanicness" created by Euroamerican ethics is reinforced and furthered by Latino/as forced to enter the discourse using the ethical paradigms that unconsciously or consciously contribute to their intellectual subjugation. The task of the Hispanic ethicist is not to leave the whiteness of empire in place undisturbed, but rather to move the conversation beyond the ethics that has been normalized and toward an indigenous liberative ethics designed to decenter both empire and the Eurocentric ethics that ignores its complicity with empire. The challenge is not so much constructing a Hispanic ethical motif as it is debunking the prevailing Eurocentric ethics that undergirds a moral world vision that makes empire possible.

We conclude that Euroamerican-based ethics will not save the Hispanic, mainly because Euroamericans do not know, nor do they need to know, what happens when baloney is fried. For ethics to be liberative, it must move beyond the ethics of the dominant culture, even when those ethics are liberal and progressive. Why? Because Euroamerican-based ethics generally either ignores or provides justification for the prevailing structures of oppression that remain detrimental to people of color. And if ethics fails to address oppressive structures, then Hispanics must construct new ethical paradigms for their communities. Those who benefit from the power and privilege accorded by the dominant culture are incapable of fashioning an objective ethical code of behavior because their standing within society is protected by the prevailing social structures. I therefore call Hispanics to move away from Euroamerican ethics that stands in opposition to the Latino/a community. Hispanics fail to consider critically how such an ethics strengthens and advances empire, and thus they fail to consider seriously their own racialization. Those white Euroamericans who wish to do Christian ethics must also move away from white ethics and, in solidarity with marginalized communities, participate in liberative praxis—that is, praxis rooted in the social location of those who know what happens when you fry baloney.

During the Republican National Convention of 1992, defeated presidential candidate Pat Buchanan took the stage to give a primetime televised call to arms: "There is a religious war going on in our country for the soul of America. It is a cultural war, as critical to the kind of nation we will one day be as was the Cold War itself."[1] Frankly, Buchanan is right. There is a battle waging between the Religious Right and the Religious Left to determine who will represent the moral voice of empire. It is as if both sides are playing that childhood game "king of the hill," disguised as righteous indignation each toward the other. Christian conservatives and liberals are collectively striving to acquire political, social, cultural, and economic power to determine the direction of the empire, but this striving is masked as a Christian crusade to rescue the soul of America from the "un-Christian" ideologies of the other side. And yet, undergirding both sides is the same hypermasculine ideology that loves power. Both sides are assigned specific roles in this power game, with conservatives defending the empire and its so-called Christian traditions, while liberals are fighting to reform the empire. Regardless of who wins the cultural wars, empire continues because neither side is calling for its dismantling. Both sides share the same moral and cultural values that privilege whiteness and either distrust or fail to understand whatever and whomever they consider foreign or alien.

Regardless of who "wins" this power game, the disenfranchisement of Hispanics will continue. Unfortunately, conservatives tend to ignore our social location while liberals tend to treat us as some romanticized icon (e.g., "they are such hardworking people belonging to a rich and noble race"). Our salvation and hope for liberation reside with neither camp. Still, because of the demographic growth of Hispanics, both sides need to curry Latina/o Christians' support if they hope to win the game.

Even though Hispanics will comprise one out of every four Americans by 2035, already now their numbers are beginning to affect U.S. policies, as evidenced by the 2008 presidential elections. During the massive 2005 Hispanic marches held throughout the country demanding a comprehensive immigration reform that did not come, a particular chant was heard on the streets of all the major U.S. cities. "*Hoy marchamos, mañana votamos.*"[2] Tomorrow came on November 4, 2008 when Hispanics, in record numbers, voted for Senator Obama at a two-to-one margin over Senator McCain. And while it may be true that since 1972, Democratic candidates have on average garnered about two-thirds of the Hispanic vote in each presidential election, what made 2008 unique is the unprecedented number of Latina/os who went to the polls. Because of the growth of the Hispanic population and changing demographics of the battleground states where that growth occurred, Latina/os had a major role in choosing the next president. These demographic changes have altered the electoral map. The sleeping giant has awakened, and the politicos have taken notice.

The growth of the Hispanic community makes them a swing vote that can no longer be ignored. According to the Census Bureau, Latino/as are responsible for about half of America's population growth between 2000 and 2006. Places like Iowa, Kansas, and North Carolina are witnessing phenomenal growth in numbers of Hispanics. What the McCain camp failed to realize is that the browning of America has made José the plumber a better signifier of who we are as a nation than Joe the plumber. The demographic shifts that have occurred and continue to occur in this nation mean that neither side of the cultural war can win the soul of America, or the votes to make their views the law of the land, without the backing of the growing U.S. Hispanic population. And as tempting as it might appear to cast our lot with the Religious Right because we share similar traditional and conservative values and beliefs, or with the Religious Left, because we share similar liberal social and political leanings, in the long run, both options might very well prove to be damaging to our moral bearings. To join either camp is to assimilate, adopting the moral framework that makes empire building possible. Besides, liberation can never be reduced to equality with white middle-class privilege. Liberation must advance full humanity for all, especially the least among us, a process that can never occur through alliance with any empire, regardless of how benevolent that empire might appear to be. As tempting and profitable as complicity with empire may be, as a people, compliance comes at the expense of our beliefs in Jesus Christ.

There are Christians who have historically merged the goals of the U.S. Empire with the Christian faith, using the latter to justify the former—a spiritual and political methodology employed by many within the Religious Right, Center, and Left. They are responsible for providing moral justification for a U.S. Christian history marked by the conquest of the land, the genocide of the indigenous populations, and the enslavement of generations of people; and, for Hispanics specifically, this history has been marked by a domestic war policy that moved the borders over Latino/as, a foreign policy based on "gunboat diplomacy," and a "Good Neighbor Policy"[3] that extracted the natural resources and labor of countries of Hispanic origin. Christians who accept empire as normative and legitimate are those who also created and participated in a history of Mexican lynching by Texas Rangers and in present day immigration policies (e.g., Operation Gatekeeper) that since 1994 are based on causing brown bodies to die horrific deaths in inhospitable terrain to deter others from making the hazardous desert crossing. And yet the Religious Right, Center, and Left, in the midst of these human rights violations, either have said little or have tried to maintain the status quo while suggesting cosmetic reforms. How then can Hispanics pledge their allegiance to either side of the cultural war? What they are warring about fails to center the moral and ethical issues crucial to *nuestra comunidad.*

No person can serve two masters, for he or she will love one and hate the other. To use faith to justify conquest is antithetical to the heart of the gospel, and to travel on that road is to deny everything Jesus taught. In the final analysis, the Religious Right who call for strengthening the U.S. Empire, and the Religious Left who call for reforming the U.S. Empire, are the two sides of the same Constantinian coin. It matters little if a conservative like George W. Bush or a liberal like Barack Obama occupies the highest office in the empire; their administrations will be co-opted, with both the Religious Right and the Religious Left (depending on who is president) cooperating with the empire. In return for their loyalty and support during the electoral process, religious leaders are allowed to carve out for themselves a sphere within the empire that allows them to influence the political process (De La Torre, 2007: 49–51).

Much can be said about the Religious Right's complicity with empire; however, that is not the purpose of this chapter. All too often, books on the cultural wars focus on the Religious Right and look toward the Religious Left as a feasible alternative. After all, the prevailing wisdom among liberal academicians is that the Religious Left is more enlightened. The Religious Right's complicity with empire, especially as demonstrated during the Reagan and Bush administrations, is well documented, as neoconservative politicians relied on the theology of the Religious Right while its religious leaders (e.g., Jerry Falwell, Pat Robertson, and James Dobson, to name a few) provided grassroots support and spiritual justification, through their ministries, to these politicians' empire-building ventures. By contrast, many from the Religious Left were, and continue to be, vocal on issues important to Latina/os—issues concerning racial and ethnic reconciliation, economic justice, and the dangers of an imperial foreign policy. Yet, I still will argue that in spite of the Religious Left's concerns about issues important to the Hispanic community, they also are complicit with empire. I will prove my assertion by reviewing the works of three of the Religious Left's most prominent voices today: Ronald J. Sider, Anthony Campolo, and Jim Wallis. And just as the previous chapter advocated moving beyond the Eurocentric ethics proceeding from the academy, this chapter advocates moving beyond the Religious Left. I will argue that the Religious Left can be more damning to the Latina/o social location than the Religious Right or Center; but before turning our attention to them, it behooves us to remind ourselves briefly why Latino/as will not find salvation with either the Religious Right or the Religious Center.

THE RELIGIOUS RIGHT AND CENTER

Many in the Religious Right tend to support a pro-U.S. theocracy that assumes its own correctness. Ironically, while many leaders of the Religious Right claim to be "born-again" Christians wishing to influence public policy away from secular humanism, in actuality, their agenda could be seen as a pro-empire, savage capitalism influenced by a nativist, expansionist ideology maintained through a racist hierarchical political structure. In effect, they promote three different forms of racism, each associated with a different subset of the Religious Right. Though dissimilar in some ways, these groups are in agreement in their attempts to protect white privilege and prevent any in-depth reconciliation across the racial and ethnic divide. As long as these forms of racism undergird the Religious Right, Hispanics will continue to lack voice or presence unless they fully assimilate to the Religious Right worldview concerning race, among other issues.

The three subsets of the Religious Right are (1) the far right, (2) the new right, and (3) the neoconservatives. According to sociologist Howard Winant, the Far Right Racial Project can be identified by two fascist elements: (1) belief in the biological superiority of whites over nonwhites (and Jews), and (2) insurrectionary posture vis-à-vis the state (2004: 53). Among the far right are individuals like Larry Pratt, who is best remembered for helping to launch the militia movement. He served as the head of Gunowners of America (which functions as a kind of liaison between the militia movement and Capitol Hill) and English First (the Hispanic-immigrant-bashing group). He also served as cochairman of Pat Buchanan's presidential campaign but was forced to resign because of his links to some of the most racist, anti-Semitic, heavily armed organizations of America's fringe far right (such as Christian Identity, whose leader Pete Peters warns that Jews are children of the devil) and because he had given videotaped speeches to Aryan Nation, skinhead, and Klansmen groups (Lamy, 1996: 259).

The New Right Racial Project, according to Winant, differs from the far right by not vocally espousing white supremacy. Unlike the far right, the new right embraces mainstream political activities. The new right can accept a few nonwhites to politically and socially participate within the prevailing power structures as long as they are willing to expound color blindness (see definition of color blindness below). Participants in this movement differ from the neoconservatives by their willingness to manipulate whites' fear of people of color through "coded language." This was best demonstrated during George Bush Sr.'s 1988 Willie Horton campaign ads and California governor Pete Wilson's attack on immigrants for electoral purposes (2004: 56–57).

And finally, Winant describes the Neoconservative Racial Project as a discourse wishing to preserve white advantages through the denial of racial differences, which for this group, as for the new right, is best accomplished by advocating color blindness (2004: 57). White resentment toward the consequences of neoliberalism is blamed on unfair advantages given to nonwhites (i.e., affirmative action), which can only be remedied when everyone is treated the same, regardless of how social structures continue to privilege whites. Establishing a color-blind society is the expressed goal of many powerful and influential leaders from the Religious Right, including Richard Viguerie, Tom DeLay, Phyllis Schlafly, Gary Bauer,[4] Joseph Coors,[5] James Dobson (whose Focus on the Family Web page celebrated Chief Justice William Rehnquist for upholding the "intent of a color-blind civil rights law"),[6] and Paul Weyrich (who sits on the board of the Houston-based Campaign for a Color-Blind America),[7] to name but a few. The problem with expounding color blindness is that regardless of Euroamericans' best intentions, the disparities between non-Hispanic whites and people of color show that social structures are not color blind.

Why must Hispanics be wary of the Religious Right? Because the philosophical underpinnings and the hermeneutical conclusions reached by the Religious Right are detrimental to the Hispanic social location. Only through assimilation can Latina/os reconcile with the empire and its religious expression designed to justify its place within the world order. Unfortunately, the new manifestations of racism elucidated by Winant demonstrate the Religious Right's complicity with racist structures and, by extension, with the empire. Nevertheless, the racial and ethnic reconciliation Hispanics seek insists that true Christianity make no provisions for racism or discrimination. Religious sociologist Antony Alumkal reminds us that the main argument of Christians, specifically conservative and evangelical Christians, is that "only through the common lordship of Christ [is] reconciliation between races possible" (2004: 198). Because Christ is Lord, the Religious Right can downplay, if not outright ignore, the importance of initiating sociopolitical acts that challenge the present social structures embedded in empire. For them, reconciliation is achieved through personal relationships across racial and ethnic lines. Stressing individual-level actions over and against changing social structures allows those who are privileged by those same structures to feel righteous because of apologies given for past racist acts. Meanwhile, they can continue to benefit from the status quo because of their Eurocentric privilege. Winant concludes his observations by claiming that the biological racism of the far right, the expedient and subtex-tual racism of the new right, and the bad-faith antiracism of the neoconservatives have many differences from each other, but they have at least one thing in common. They all seek to maintain the long-standing associations between whiteness and U.S. political traditions, between whiteness and U.S. nationalism, between whiteness and universalism. (2004: 66)

Unfortunately, the Religious Center fails to provide any feasible alternative. According to David Gushee, who situates himself in the Center, this is an emerging group that attempts to find some middle ground between the Right and the Left. But like the Religious Right, the Religious Center allows no room for Hispanics. Although the Center can be commended for concerns about the poor and an emphasis on eliminating racism and protecting human rights, their approach is still deeply rooted in the empire and thus falls short of providing any liberative hope for Latina/os. For example, according to Gushee, the Religious Center prefers to speak about racial reconcili-ation rather than racial justice (2008: 89), thus ignoring what mar-ginalized communities of color have always been saying, that there can be no reconciliation without justice. Cheap reconciliation, which costs those privileged by the present social structures nothing, costs those on their underside everything, because they remain subject to institutionalized violence. Apologies are meaningless if there is no radical change within the social structures to bring about justice.

On economic ethics, the Religious Center, according to Gushee, has not embraced antiglobalization or anti-free trade. Instead, its sympathies remain with the current practice of global capitalism. In other words, the Religious Center remains committed to neolib-eralism, the global economic structure that maintains and sustains the American position of power in the world by having the world's resources disproportionately flowing toward the empire's center to the detriment of what Fanon would call "The Wretched of the Earth." In Gushee's own words: "On the issue of America's role in the world, the center tends to be much more muted in its overall criticism than the left. It does not generally accept or employ the language of 'American imperialism'" (2008: 90).

We can conclude that for Hispanics, the Religious Right and the Religious Center are not really that far apart. In the final analysis, the Right and Center remain too complicit with empire. If Hispanic ethicists are unable to find a home within the Religious Right or Center, does it mean that their only alternative is the Religious Left? I will argue, No. Although concerns over similar social issues can lead to joint strategic cooperation between Hispanics and the Religious Left, it does not mean that Latina/os must throw in their lot with the Religious Left, for it too, in the final analysis, is complicit with empire and thus must be dealt with cautiously.

THE RELIGIOUS LEFT

No doubt Latina/os and the Religious Left can agree on some matters, specifically in areas concerning the eradication of poverty and a more inclusive approach to the accessibility of social services, issues that disproportionately affect Latina/os. Still, as attractive as the Religious Left may appear, its ultimate goal is to "reform" the empire, not redistribute power or wealth. A "kinda, gentla" empire remains an empire.

When Euroamerican liberals join in solidarity with people of color concerning issues crucial to dispossessed communities, some liberals still refuse to place justice over social order. Let us not forget that it was the liberal, progressive clergy's criticism of Martin Luther King Jr.'s timing for his organized march that led King to write his famous "Letter from Birmingham Jail" (1964). No doubt, the eight religious leaders to whom King formally addressed his famous letter were among the few white residents of Birmingham who publicly opposed Governor Wallace's defiance of federal desegregation orders. Still, King recognized that the greatest stumbling block to freedom was not the hooded Ku Klux Klan member, but the co-option of any liberationist movement by well-meaning Euroamericans who would deradicalize the movement's goals to make it more palatable to Euroamerican sensibilities. According to King, the greatest threat to liberation is

> the white moderate who is more devoted to "order" than to justice . . . who constantly says: "I agree with you in the goal you seek, but I cannot agree with your methods of direct action"; who paternalistically believes he can set the timetable for another man's freedom. . . . Shallow understanding from people of good will is more frustrating than absolute misunderstanding from people of ill will. Lukewarm acceptance is much more bewildering than outright rejection. (1964: 84–85)

King understood that well-meaning liberals were quick to profess solidarity with noble concepts like equality, justice, and dignity for the marginalized, but that when it came to actually implementing social change, they tended to discourage praxis that could threaten their privileged positions within the social structures and/or upset the societal equilibrium that provided them and their families with security.

The concern for Latino/as doing liberative ethics from within the Religious Left is that whenever the marginalized organize to bring about change, well-meaning liberals, with "a shallow understanding" of the Hispanic social location, soon co-opt the movement and in so doing make the demands less radical, making liberation an illusion—an illusion that will persist unless the privileged status that creates inequalities is first rectified. If truth be known, I am less concerned with the neoconservatives, for if a tree is known by its fruits, then those residing on the underside of power are all too familiar with the produce hanging from its limbs. It is the Euroamerican liberal and progressive politicians, clergy, ethicists, and activists that can prove to be the most dangerous, for their fruits may be pleasing to the eye because of their justice rhetoric, but they can be as damaging to the welfare of the oppressed as their neoconservative counterparts. Regardless of how Christian or sincere they appear, their acceptance of benefits from the empire that privileges them ultimately places them at odds with the liberationist hopes and aspirations of the oppressed. Liberals may demonstrate compassion toward Hispanics, but when all is said and done, like neoconservatives, most will employ whatever means are necessary to secure the interests of empire and the privileged space it safeguards. It matters not that holders of political or social power are guided by Eurocentric ethical principles based on leftist thought: absent from the discourse is how to dismantle the global interests of IBM, General Motors, Walmart, or Coca-Cola.

While much has been written concerning the political clout of the Religious Right, especially from 1980 through 2008, the Religious Left, in comparison, appears lackluster. It lacks a corporate institutional base from which to draw resources, an ecclesiastical institutional base from which to rally an army of grassroots volunteers, or widely recognized charismatic spokespersons to articulate the Religious Left mission and vision. It has neither the unity, the size, nor the political connections of a Southern Baptist Convention, nor an unofficial coalition of nondenominational megachurches to provide support to the Democratic Party and serve as the moral voice of America. Nevertheless, some, motivated by their faith, have challenged the Religious Right's attempt to be the sole voice of Christianity in America. They hope to move the morality discourse away from personal piety (specifically the two major issues of abortion and homosexuality) by emphasizing conversations on social justice. One example is the Network of Spiritual Progressives (NSP);[8] however, lack of corporate financial resources prevents them from truly competing with the multiple political action committees associated with the Religious Right.

When we consider the intersection of religiosity and political activism, it is difficult to identify an organized Religious Left. While the political machinery of the Republican Party has made room for the Religious Right, the machinery of the Democratic Party is reluctant to accommodate any religious organization, including the Religious Left, taking great pains to maintain the wall of separation between government and religion. For many on the political left, religion (if it is important) should remain an individual conviction, best kept out of the public arena. Nevertheless, after George W. Bush's 2004 electoral victory, some of the Democratic Party leadership reached out to the Religious Left for assistance in finding their religious voice when opining on major issues facing the nation.[9] Unfortunately, while the Religious Right has mastered the "sound bite," the Religious Left appears more academic, constantly nuancing their comments and seeming too obliging to diverse (and at times unpopular) views.

We will employ the same methodology here as in the previous chapter, turning our attention to the writings and activism of three prominent religious leaders associated with the Religious Left: Ron Sider, Tony Campolo, and Jim Wallis. Although these three religious activists are constantly linked to "the Religious Left" by the media and by the Religious Right, the label might be a bit of a misnomer.[10] Some would argue they are closer to the center-to-left, while others, myself included, would see them as closer to moderate conservatives. Because most true leftists are not necessarily associated with religious movements, and may even be suspicious of them, perhaps these three best capture the activism of Christians who are simply left of the Religious Right. Although Sider, Campolo, and Wallis hold conservative theological views, they advocate a more liberal political agenda (except in the area of abortion and gay rights). Regardless of where these men fall, no one questions their commitment to justice or the good they hope to accomplish. All three should be congratulated for the praxis-based ethics in which they participate, which is more than can be said about most liberal or progressive academic ethicists. They should be recognized for calling Christians to live physically with the poor, so they can learn from them, and to give according to the needs of the poor. Because they stand in solidarity with the oppressed, a multitude of sins can be covered. Yet, as much as they may deserve praise, and as much as they may be allies on some issues important to Hispanics, the ethical framework from which they operate must ultimately be critiqued, because they either support the empire or have a "shallow understanding" of the Hispanic experience, and thus fall short of liberation. I will attempt to elucidate this point by investigating a small yet adequate representation of their works.

RONALD J. SIDER

We begin our exploration with Ronald J. Sider, professor of theology and culture at Palmer Theological Seminary in Wynnewood, Pennsylvania, and founder of Evangelicals for Social Action (1973). He is a scholar-activist who for years has challenged the materialism of evangelicals by applying biblical insights to contemporary social issues, specifically economic issues. He attempts to merge the conservative emphasis of personal salvation with social concerns of liberals to move beyond what he calls a "one-sided Christianity," toward what he calls a "wholistic theology" based on both liberal activism—reforming social structures—and conservative evangelicalism (1993: 25). But in reality, this wholistic theology is a gentler form of empire theology, for while Sider decries the abuses of colonialism, he ultimately redeems it because the colonial venture accomplishes the all-crucial role of "saving" the heathens from their sins through their acceptance of Jesus Christ as their Lord and Savior. Specifically he writes,

> It would be simplistic, of course, to suggest that the impact of colonialism and subsequent economic and political relations with industrialized nations was entirely negative. It was not. Among other things, literacy rates rose and health care improved. I also thank God that opportunities to spread the gospel around the

world increased during the colonial period. But think of how different colonial history would be if missionaries had challenged imperial injustice more often. Christian values sometimes undercut ancient social evils, such as the caste system in India, but what a tragedy that so much of the impact of the "Christian" North on the developing political and economic structures of the colonies was shaped by economic self-interest rather than the biblical principles of justice. If the whole biblical message had been shared and lived in social and economic life, developing nations would know less misery today. If Christian attitudes toward property and wealth had ruled the colonizers' actions . . . there would be less need for this book [*Rich Christians in an Age of Hunger*] today. (1997: 135)

Sider's apologetics for empire theology is troublesome for multiple reasons. Let's ignore the fact that the caste system as employed in India during the colonial venture was reformulated by the British overlords to subdue the vast majority of the population by privileging a small indigenous elite.[11] Also, let us not dwell on how the Hindu faith is "a major cause of poverty in India," but the Christian empire was able to save heathens from such "unbiblical worldviews" (1997: 126). Instead, let us focus on how Sider's understanding of empire building is problematic because of its overarching emphasis on spiritually saving pagans over against them being physically ground up under the machinery of empire. He takes seriously the evangelical mission to spread the gospel of individual born-again salvation to the entire world. Not only must Christians work to eradicate poverty as an outward expression of their inward conversion, but if global poverty is to be effectively reduced, then the poor must also accept Christ as their personal Savior. For Sider, there can be no social justice if there is no conversion to Christ. "[Because] the problem lies deeper than mere social systems and is located finally in distorted human hearts, personal spiritual conversion is also essential for long-term societal improvement" (1999: 54). Sider does not unequivocally denounce empire but proposes how empire could do God's work if it would be Christianized by following biblical principles of justice, a utopian concept never realized in the centuries of colonialism. Empire building, to Sider, is morally neutral. It can be a force for good or bad, depending on the Christian commitment of the colonizer. If the colonizer is shaped by what Sider calls "economic self-interest," then the colonial venture will result in "misery." But, he wonders, what could that venture have been if it had been based on "biblical principles of justice"? Then there would be no need for him to write a book about global poverty, because it would not exist. When empires are Christian, they serve God's divine purpose of protecting the rights of those oppressed by the powerful, and thus are a necessity to be embraced (1999: 71–73). He seems to ignore that empire tends to protect the rights of the powerful at the expense of the weak. His shortsightedness concerning the colonized is best revealed when he praises the U.S.' long history of implementing governmental policy to create wealth among its citizens. He cites how Thomas Jefferson made public land available to farmers who were willing to work the land, forgetting that this so-called public land was stolen from the original indigenous inhabitants. To make the land "public" before passing it on to farmers as private, those on the land had to be either removed or exterminated. Thomas Jefferson and preceding presidents gravitated toward the latter option. Sider may biblically sanction private property (1997: 91–92), but apparently he will not sanction Native American and Chicano/a rights to the land.

Besides embracing empire when operated on biblical principles by Christians, Sider also embraces neoliberalism. He does a superb job of showing racial and ethnic inequalities in society, but when he asks why they exist, not only does he fail to consider the role neoliberalism plays, he endorses it as the best economic alternative. "The twentieth century has taught us that market economies are more efficient than socialist economies. They also strengthen freedom. A biblical view of persons and sin also leads to the conclusion that market economies offer a better framework than present alternatives" (1999: 87). He chooses capitalism over the socialist alternatives, not because it is more just, but because it is "more efficient," thus elevating efficiency above justice in his ethics. He looks to corporations founded by Christians to prove that biblical principles and what Pope John Paul II called "savage capitalism" can be reconciled. But Sider's examples focus on the faith of the company's founders rather than on those on the underside of the corporations. While he praises a company like Merry Maids for its corporate defined management objectives to "honor God [and] help people develop," he fails to include the perspectives of those who are actually cleaning the houses as maids (116). He does ethics/theology from on top.

But how would companies like Merry Maids fare if examined from the margins? From the location of those who dust and vacuum? As famed investigative author Barbara Ehrenreich, who took a job with a maid service company, demonstrates, company objectives do not necessarily translates well for those at the bottom rung of the corporation (2001: 51–120).

If Sider had been conscientized to the plight of the colonized, it would have been almost impossible for him to justify any aspect of empire building as beneficial. Rather than dealing with a majority of voices of color that questions present social structures, Sider tends to create caricatures of the marginalized. In reading his books one gets the impression that the only black people he knows are angry.[12] Fortunately, they were "born again" and then adopted, as their own, Sider's Eurocentric understanding of Jesus and the biblical text. They are no longer angry, having gotten over something Sider calls "white racism." For Sider, racism is a synonym for prejudice or bias. Missing is any critical race or power analysis.

Sider's overall work attempts to find a middle ground between the so-called liberal position that social "structures and systematic injustices" contribute to poverty and the so-called conservative position that "poverty has result[ed] from wrong moral choices exacerbated by bad government policy" (1999: 35). Both, in his mind, are equally responsible for U.S. poverty. But by making the disenfranchised also responsible for their poverty, he proves their moral inferiority, and thus implies that people of color, who are disproportionately represented among the dispossessed, are also morally inferior. But privileged Euroamericans and dispossessed persons of color are not equally responsible. If a Euroamerican makes poor moral choices, she or he faces a more forgiving judicial system, has better access to social services that can provide a safety net, and is more likely to have the class privilege necessary to cushion the consequences. Furthermore, Sider ignores the numerous studies that show how normative racist structures contribute to poor moral choices by the disenfranchised. Sider may see "structures and systematic injustices" and "wrong moral choices" as connected and needing equal attention, but he fails to see how the former often contribute to the latter.

It is interesting to note that Sider critiques evangelical theology through the use of liberationist themes, insisting that God *is* on the side of the poor, but in the final analysis he is no liberationist.[13] For

Sider, salvation is not liberation. He fails adequately to tie economic poverty to the sin of oppression and therefore fails to tie salvation to liberation from that oppression. To be saved, as far as Sider, as a representative of the one true faith, is concerned, is to be "born again." Salvation comes by adopting a white Protestant middle-class evangelical interpretation and definition of what is moral—which is okay if one is a white Protestant middle-class evangelical, but most of the world is not. Furthermore, salvation language is only for those who respond positively to Jesus. To move this language to encompass God's working or kingdom activity taking place outside the church, as do liberationists, contradicts for Sider the biblical text. According to Sider:

> Salvation language . . . should not be used to talk about the growth of freedom and justice in human society beyond the church when Christians and non-Christians alike create more free, just, social systems. To be sure, people who adopt the narrower view of salvation insist strongly that Christians should combat social sin and change unjust structures. They believe that Christian faith has powerful "spill-over" effect in the larger society. But we should call the result justice, freedom, and environmental wholeness, not salvation. (1993: 199–200)

Regardless of whether or not he limits salvation to born-again evangelicals, he is to be commended for insisting that any faith that claims to be Christian must feed the hungry, provide drink to the thirsty, clothe the naked, take in the alien within our midst, attend to the ill, and visit the incarcerated. While this gospel-based praxis resonates with Hispanic liberationist ethicists, Sider's other interpretations of Scripture remain problematic. Part of the concern is that the praxis Sider institutes is based on what he believes to be a "clear teaching of Scripture" (1993: 133): "If we want to be biblical, however, we must submit to scriptural norms even when they contradict our inherited biases and ideological preferences" (1999: 50). Solely on the basis of God's word he is able to conclude that correct praxis is aligned with God's will. He is so sure his interpretations are correct that he challenges the reader to "just explain clearly to me how the normative biblical framework I spell out is not adequately scripture" (15). Gladly! Sider, like the rest of us, reads Scripture from a particular social location. What is "normative" for him is not Scripture, but what his culture and upbringing have taught him that

Scripture says. He fuses and confuses the biblical text with what he thinks the Bible says.[14] If I, too, were a Euroamerican or an assimilated Hispanic, I also would agree that Sider's interpretations are normative. But I am not; hence, how he reads Scripture may be an interesting Eurocentric perspective, but it is irrelevant, if not dangerous, for Latino/as and the Hispanic ethos.

ANTHONY CAMPOLO

Anthony Campolo is Professor Emeritus of Sociology at Eastern University and founder of the Evangelical Association for the Promotion of Education, and he was a spiritual advisor to President Bill Clinton during the Monica Lewinsky affair. Like Sider, Campolo believes his mission is to "help build the Kingdom of God by combining evangelism and social justice in the name of Christ" (Gushee, 2008: 61). But his attempt to bridge this gap, like Sider's, fails to consider seriously how empire actually works. This is most obvious in how he defines power.

For Campolo, power is "the prerogative to determine what happens and the coercive force to make others yield to your wishes—*even against their own will*" (1984: 11; emphasis original). Any liberative Hispanic ethics we hope to construct must have a more sophisticated analysis of power than simply coercion; specifically, attention must be given to the extent power is legitimized and normalized within society. In the final chapter of this book we will explore this theme more closely; but for now, it is important to see why Campolo's simplistic understanding of power is not liberative for Latina/os, and in spite of his heart's desire to stand in solidarity with dispossessed communities, his definition of power at times further contributes to their marginalization.

Campolo is very critical about the negative influence the U.S. has had on other nations; nevertheless, his failure to move beyond romanticizing the U.S. and its people limits alternatives he can suggest to challenge the dominant position the U.S. as empire occupies in the world. In the opening pages of his book *Wake Up, America!* preceding the title page, appears a reprinted brochure in which Campolo challenges the reader to "recapture the sacredness of our national character." He goes on to claim that America's Christians are the ones who hold the key to change. Specifically,

> Christians in America enjoy an unprecedented opportunity. We are the wealthiest group of believers in all history. Our privilege

and power far exceed that of any other generation. And we bear
an awesome responsibility to help direct the resources of our great
country into efforts that will help heal our nation and our world.
(1991: i)

Missing from Campolo's analysis is how "we" became the wealthi-
est group of believers, a status achieved specifically because there
was no "sacred character." Campolo reinforces and perpetuates the
liberal myth that the founding of the United States was based on
the noble ideal of religious freedom and democratic principles. Elsewhere, he and coauthor Gordon Aeschliman recognize a misguided
church that participated in ethnic oppression and, specifically, "con-
doned the mistreatment of Native Americans," in a chapter titled
"Helping Those New to Our Land." But ironically, he confuses "mistreatment" with genocide and land theft, and he calls the church
to "love the foreigner and the stranger," missing the point that it is
the Europeans who are the foreigners (2006: 137–39). The failure
to connect the wealth of North Americans with the genocide of
Native Americans to steal their lands, the enslavement of African
Americans to steal their bodies, and the pauperization of Latino/
as to steal their labor leads to a romanticized Christian America
that ignores how this political entity was constructed on ideologies
fostering white supremacy, Manifest Destiny, savage capitalism, and
colonialism. These ideologies constitute what Campolo terms "the
sacredness of our national character," which he hopes to recapture.

The Religious Left may be critical of the U.S.' use of power
throughout the world, but like the Religious Right, it fails to recognize that there is very little that is sacred about our national character. U.S. Empire emerged during the start of the twentieth century
(as discussed in the previous chapter) on the basis of a capitalism
developed by stealing resources of the countries of origin of U.S.
Hispanics through gunboat diplomacy and the Good Neighbor
Policy. So-called undeveloped nations can never be developed following the U.S. model because they have no one to enslave or colo-
nize. Additionally, while many factors led to the failure of the 1960s
Alliance for Progress program; it did demonstrate that Two-Thirds
World nations can never be lifted to the levels of development of the
U.S. because the earth simply lacks sufficient resources to make this
happen (Smith, 1991: 111–15).

Both Campolo and Sider take empire for granted. The mechanisms that cause an unequal distribution of the earth's resources

do not appear relevant in their discourse; take for example the title of a chapter in one of Campolo's books: "How to Be Rich and Still Be a Christian." Although the chapter provides some sound practical advice, it never asks, how did the person become rich? Campolo does not make the connection between the riches of a few and the poverty of many. Instead, he concludes that the rich just know how to make money and the poor do not (1997: 9–19)—a problematic conclusion when we consider the race and ethnicity of many of those who are poor. The answer therefore cannot be that the poor need to learn how to be like the rich, that is, that Latino/as must learn how to be Euroamericans.

Also missing from Campolo's analysis is the empire's hunger for resources from Hispanics' lands of origin. Although he recognizes the devastation that cash crops have upon food crops (1985: 163), he misses how the empire's demand for cash crops perpetuates economic hardships responsible for our immigration into the empire's entrails. Where is the analysis of poverty caused by foreign agreements like NAFTA? The focus is upon reforming the structures, using neoliberalism to bring liberation to the world's disenfranchised. The Christian economic system he envisions is based on free enterprise motivated by love, not motivated by profits. It meets the needs of the people rather than seeking the maximization of production. It is a system that transcends the competitiveness of capitalism (175–76).

This vision of a love-based neoliberalism fails to challenge the global mechanisms that funnel the vast resources and labor of Two-Thirds World nations (many of which are U.S. Latino/as' countries of origin) to the center of the empire. Campolo believes the global structures should be reformed through the creation of cottage industries in these countries:

> Eastern [the institution where Campolo taught] started a graduate program to train a new generation of missionaries to be catalysts for ecologically sound entrepreneurial ventures around the world. Scores of graduates from Eastern are already out on the mission field, serving the poor by helping them start businesses and cottage industries that indigenous people will own and run. . . . Graduates of Eastern's program know that the best way to fight poverty in the Third World is by creating jobs for the poor. (1992: 115–16)

No one disputes that the creation of microindustries is excellent praxis. Nor is the success of some who help create them denied. But doesn't neoliberalism prevent such microbusinesses from fully developing and prospering? Is the "best way to fight poverty" really teaching indigenous people capitalism? Were not the globalization of the economy and the foreign policies of the empire that manipulates global markets for its own benefit responsible for much of the world's poverty today? If all that is recommended is creating cottage industries without seriously analyzing the illusions and consequences of neoliberalism, then all that is accomplished is providing a temporary remedy to the symptoms of poverty without dealing with its root causes.

Rather than addressing injustices caused by neoliberalism, Campolo, like Sider, believes the present economic systems can be reformed. This becomes evident in an example he provides concerning the Dominican Republic. Campolo recognizes that the multinational corporation Gulf and Western gained control of the Dominican Republic's sugar production when the U.S. Marines invaded the island in 1965. He also recognizes that Dominicans working for Gulf and Western were economically exploited—not paid enough to feed their families. How does he respond? During the 1970s, he (along with the Adrian Sisters Order) buys a few shares of stock in the company. This entitles him and the nuns to attend stockholder meetings. At these meetings they raise the consciousness of the company stockholders by depicting the economic abuse faced by their foreign employees. After a few contentious stockholder meetings, the company relents and helps develop a network of village schools and a university. They also participate in establishing medical clinics and help diversify the sugar-based economy through "industrial zones." They commit $100 million per year for five years toward the social and economic development of the island (2003: 110). These changes led Campolo to exclaim, "It is fair to say that, over the years, Gulf and Western has moved significantly toward becoming the kind of principality and power that does the will of God when it comes to economic justice" (2000b: 254).

No question that Campolo's approach of buying stock in the company was ingenious, allowing him and the nuns to better the lives of Dominicans slightly. But by insisting on the reformation of neoliberalism, Campolo misses the obvious. The land and sugar production were violently stolen from the Dominicans through an unjust and unprovoked U.S. military invasion in 1965. This invasion prevented the left-leaning president, Juan Bosch, who was elected democratically in 1962, from returning to office after being removed through a military coup. The U.S. invasion assured U.S. political and economic control over the island—a control maintained by the death squads (known as *La Banda*) established by the U.S.-backed government shortly after the invasion. By 1970 *La Banda* averaged one death every thirty-four hours. The invasion allowed Gulf and Western to become the largest private landowner (8% of all arable land, mainly in sugar) and employer in the country, owning a large resort complex and having investments in some ninety Dominican businesses. The "industrial zones" Campolo celebrates provided companies with a ten-year tax-free status, gun-toting law-enforcement officers to maintain order by breaking up union strikes and "disappearing" union leaders, and finally, a work facility the AFL-CIO describes as a "modern slave-labor camp" (Chomsky and Herman, 1979: 242–48).

What is puzzling about Campolo's praising the corporate practices of Gulf and Western for significantly moving toward doing the will of God is that he is aware of the damage done by such multinational companies. Elsewhere he wrote, "Our economic system is not necessarily of benefit to all other nations. Try tracing the consequences of what some of our multinational corporations have done in Latin America, and you will discover negative effects that, in many cases, outweigh any good they have done" (1985: 62). And yet he misses how the U.S. invasion turned the Dominican Republic into the "company country" of Gulf and Western. By 1984, Gulf and Western had sold all of its holdings in the Dominican Republic. By the next year, the company had produced $3.7 billion and controlled $7 billion in assets, more than doubling the price of their stock. Consider that in 1965 (the year of the invasion), company annual sales barely reached $200,000;[15] it is fair to say that acquiring and then selling Santo Domingo was very profitable to the company. But it is not fair to say, as Campolo does, that Gulf and Western is doing "the will of God."

Gulf and Western was the economic arm of the empire in Santo Domingo that stole and killed to maintain the power and privilege of the center. Campolo's attempt to show how an empire can be benevolent and how neoliberalism can be godly fails because he refuses to approach Santo Domingo from the social location of the

Dominicans. The construction of a few schools and clinics, in the final analysis, is "chump change" compared to all that Gulf and Western stole with the backing of the empire. Half a billion dollars over five years does not begin to compensate for stolen land, stolen labor, stolen means of production, or stolen lives. Why doesn't Campolo instead discuss returning what has been stolen? And to complicate this analysis, we must also ask why the Dominican population within the U.S. is drastically increasing, soon to surpass Cubans as the third largest Hispanic population in the United States. Could it be that they are following the labor and goods (sugars) stolen from them since the U.S. invasion of their island? How then do a few school buildings and clinics built on the island begin to provide restitution for expatriation? What these questions reveal is Campolo's simplistic understanding of empire and neoliberalism, which leads him to confuse public relations stunts implemented by multinational corporations with their conversion to doing God's will and thus finding God's favor.

No doubt, there is in Campolo's writings some recognition of the horrors done in the past to communities of color. Nevertheless, he continues to take a paternalistic approach to moving forward, an approach that seems to put the burden on marginalized communities. For example, he tells a story about a white Dutch college student who was teaching black children the song "Ebony and Ivory." In this story, it was the black children that had to be broken of "their stereotypes" and "overcome racial differences," not the white Dutch college student (2000a: 119–20). Elsewhere he writes, "Black people often resent white people. When they do not, it is only because they have, through the grace of God, developed a very special capacity to forgive those whom they have every right to resent. . . . Resentment is still a sin and they need to escape it by the grace of God" (1984: 142). This passage is troublesome because it reduces the plight of the marginalized to resentment (not much different from Sider's "angry blacks"). How much richer would Campolo's analysis be if instead of dismissing African Americans' state of being as resentment, he had explored the pang felt by the marginalized who are forced to bear unbearable injustices. This inexpressible knot felt in the pit of their stomachs encompasses the gut feelings of helplessness, bitterness, sorrow, and yes, resentment. As such, this feeling (which Asian Americans call *han*[16]), becomes the daily companion of the powerless, the voiceless, the marginalized, and it is not limited to the individual but is experienced by the entire disenfranchised community. What Campolo misunderstands as resentment is the accumulation of generations of social injustices prevailing throughout the whole community, lacking any avenue of release or cleansing. This collective unconsciousness is not a sin, as Campolo insists; hence it cannot be resolved through God's grace, nor should it be. Resolution of what Campolo calls resentment, but what marginalized groups recognize as a collective unconsciousness, can be achieved only through a reconciliation that recognizes the causes of the continuing "resentment," correcting the wrongs by dismantling oppressive social structures.

Rather than recognizing the collective reality of the disenfranchised and the role played by the prevailing social structures in fostering this marginalization, religious leaders like Campolo find it easier to reduce the feelings of the marginalized to resentment or anger—paternalistically admonishing the oppressed that they are not *really* Christian because such feelings persist. Condemning the oppressed for unrepented resentment or anger allows the dominant culture to ignore the depths of the grievances that exist. It therefore becomes necessary to find conversation partners among *color folk* of like mind who because they know Jesus are neither angry nor resentful. Hence there is a rush toward reconciliation without needing to deal with justice, correcting the wrong, dealing with restitution. This "forgive and forget" methodology provides the empire with the opportunity of not having to change radically its structures.

And finally, like Sider, Campolo places Christianity over and against other indigenous religious expressions. Eurocentric Christianity must remain globally superior. Expressions like "In the struggle for minds and hearts of this generation, we [Christians] cannot yield anything to Buddhism" (1992: 100) or "What troubles me was that these readings [from *Black Elk Speaks*, on the spiritual relationship between Native Americans and nature] were treated as though they possessed more truth than the Bible" smack of a spiritual triumphalism that contributes to seeing the religious Other as lacking and in need of being converted to how Euroamericans understand the divine.

JIM WALLIS

The third and final figure from the Religious Left to be considered is Jim Wallis, who serves as editor of *Sojourners*, a Christian magazine that focuses on social issues, and leads a small community by the same name. J. Philip Wogaman is correct in asserting that Jim Wallis, through his publication of *Sojourners*, more than anyone else, is responsible for the 1990s evangelical "Call to Renewal." Although marketed as a created third way between the traditional politics of the right and left, Call to Renewal's main purpose is to provide an alternative to the Religious Right, helping to forge a new way of doing politics in America (2000: 131).

There is no question that the early Wallis was radical. His first book, *Agenda for Biblical People*, presents a vivid portrait of what it means to be a radical Christian, a Christian cognizant of how conservative and liberal religious expressions justify existing political and social structures (1976: 42–55). We see this same radicalism in the first issue of the forerunner of *Sojourners*, named *PostAmerican*, on whose cover Wallis placed a picture of Jesus wrapped in the American flag. The caption read, "And they crucified him." Wallis' message was clear: American Christianity was again crucifying Jesus. In one of the early editorials of the magazine, Wallis writes,

> America is a fallen nation. . . . If we had believed the Bible, we would not ignore the oppression of the poor, we would not have resisted the facts of Vietnam, we would not have been surprised by Watergate. The chaos, the insanity, the brutality that is America can only be adequately explained by the biblical doctrine of the fall: the alienation of the whole of creation from God.[17]

America's actions in the world were a demonstration of what Wallis repeatedly called the "arrogance of power."[18] He captures the essence of empire building when in 1975 he writes,

> The reason for the bloody American policies in Indochina has been the belief among policy makers that a viable, non-communist, pro-American government in the South of Vietnam is essential to the interests of the United States in the kind of world order which American policy makers are committed to. . . . Few have questioned the commitment to the kind of world order where American business, diplomatic, and military interests predominate.[19]

And when the United States elected a self-proclaimed "born-again" president in 1976, Wallis was quick to point out, correctly, how power operates.

Instead of the born-again populist peanut farmer we were prom-
ised, it seems we have gotten yet another president who is both a
creature and a captive of the not-so-born-again power structure
that has been running America for a very long time. We should
have learned by now that while presidents come and presidents
go, the real power in this country rarely changes . . . [Carter] has
effectively restored the corporate ruling class to health and office
. . . those who had power still have it and those who didn't still
don't.[20]

More than others (e.g., Sider and Campolo), Wallis is conscious of
the U.S. Empire and how it works to maintain its supremacy at the
expense of the Two-Thirds World. According to David Gushee,

Wallis suggests that one of the most pernicious developments of
the war [in Iraq] has been a creeping Pax Americana, an open
affirmation of the United States as a righteous empire, with President Bush adding a Christian theological dimension that edges
in the direction of the long-rejected Christian crusade theology.
(2008: 68)

Wallis accomplishes a sophisticated study of the merging of empire
and God in his 2003 article "George W. Bush's Theology of Empire."[21]
    Yet ironically, with the election of Barack Obama,[22] Wallis moves
away from his prophetic power analysis of empire and embraces its
elected representative (because he is black?), ignoring the fact that
regardless of race, Obama, like Carter before him, is still committed to "the not-so-born-again power structure that has been running
America," specifically Wallis states, "Most elections are just power
rearrangements; this one was a transformational moment in our history . . . a moment to recognize that fundamental shifts are taking place in America—political, cultural, racial, generational, and
religious shifts."[23] It appears that even though the Wallis of 1977
attempted to provide a prophetic voice, the Wallis of 2009 is willing
to work within the empire, believing that the election of a black man
can bring about reform. Unfortunately, Wallis mistakenly lumps
Latino/a Christians with this "new faith coalition,"[24] ignoring that
many Hispanics were and still are leery of Obama, as demonstrated
by the Latino/a vote for Clinton during the primaries. For many
Hispanics, Obama demonstrated during the primaries, and has continued to demonstrate since taking office, a lack of understanding

concerning the Hispanic social location, specifically in connection with the most important issue affecting them, immigration and the ethnic discrimination that surrounds it.

Wallis buys into the postracist rhetoric that has emerged since the election of Obama. Since the 2008 election, Euroamericans, especially liberals and progressives, have proudly proclaimed that we achieved a postracist and postsexist society, for how can we be racist or sexist when whites voted for a black man, a Latino (Bill Richardson), and a white woman in record numbers? The 2008 election cycle provided the illusion that as a country we "arrived," even though the country's distribution of income and opportunities will still fall along racial, ethnic, and gender lines. What Wallis failed to ask in his "A New Faith Coalition" article is, What did Barack Obama and John McCain (as well as Hillary Clinton and Bill Richardson) continue to have in common? All four are ontologically white males. One cannot become the leader of the world's most powerful empire unless one is committed to what male whiteness has historically symbolized within the colonial process. Saying that Obama and Richardson are ontologically white or that Clinton is ontologically male has little to do with race or gender. The question is not whether Obama is "black enough," whether Richardson is Latino enough, or whether Clinton became too masculine in order to play with the "good ol' boys" in the Senate. Such speculations are nonsensical chatter that occurred mainly among white media pundits who failed to understand the depths of this so-called historic election. Instead, Obama's and Richardson's whiteness or Clinton's maleness raised postcolonial concerns and questions.

The power of corporate monies contributed to candidates subjugates the collective will of feminists and communities of color regardless of whether "one of their own" won the election. The real ethical question to ponder is how soft monies and PACs (political action committees) subvert and pervert the proper relationship between economics and electoral democracies. It does not matter whether a black man, a Hispanic, or a white woman is elected president. If the national politics and economics of the captains of industry were to be threatened in any way with a reversal caused by the needs of U.S. marginalized communities, be they blacks, Latino/as, women, or poor whites, any future president would rally all the forces at his or her disposal to maintain the prevailing economic power structures that exist, even if those structures are detrimental to communities that share the president's gender, ethnicity, or skin pigmentation.

On the international scene, regardless of who is elected president, it would be her or his job to protect the interests of the empire abroad, as Obama made clear in his Nobel Peace prize acceptance speech. Therefore, in terms of U.S. global economic policies, it really does not matter if we elect a black man, a white woman, or a Hispanic. At this point, our democratic system has reduced our choice to two proempire individuals representing two political parties who demonstrated in their political campaigns no significant difference in their commitments to protecting the rights of multinational companies to expand financially.

During the 2008 Democratic race for the nomination, Obama, Richardson, and Clinton all ignored issues crucial to the Hispanic community, of which immigration (not the candidates' fluency in Spanish) was the most important. Additionally, the candidates did not focus upon the growing gap between the rich and poor, which has more than doubled between 1980 and 2005, a change that disproportionately affects Latina/o communities. All three candidates defended free-market policies that create greater poverty in Hispanics' nations of origin, and none of them seriously addressed the undemocratic distribution of wealth, resources, and privileges in this country. In the final analysis, they will be the black, female, or Hispanic faces of a neoliberalism that continues to privilege the few at the expense of the vast majority of the world's population.

This type of analysis, which would normally be expected from Wallis, seems to be missing. Could Wallis' new political role since the 2008 election have led him to be more accommodating to the empire? Since 2006, Wallis has moved from political "outsider" toward "insider." In his best-selling *God's Politics: Why the Right Gets It Wrong and the Left Doesn't Get It*, Wallis tries to move beyond the "red-blue" impasse. He hopes his book sparks a new dialogue, but a dialogue among whom? A dialogue among the powerful elite of both parties, a dialogue in which the Hispanic voice continues to be absent? Gushee believes, and I agree, that since the publication of *God's Politics*, Wallis has been in great demand by the Democratic Party as a political strategist, helping the party win back moderate-to-progressive religious voters (2008: 84). How can anyone be a pragmatic political strategist and a prophet? His support of Obama won him a coveted insider spot as one of the five spiritual advisors to the president.[25] Wallis' new role as spiritual advisor to the empire's commander in chief undermines his ability to represent the radical Christianity for which he called earlier in his ministry, especially when we see how the so-called radical Reverend Jeremiah White was treated when his views conflicted with the president's need to garner electoral votes.

Jim Wallis' writings (as well as the writings of Sider and Campolo) fail to consider seriously voices of U.S. Hispanics theorizing about their own social location. Any perusal of Wallis' published works, whether books or magazine editorials, finds no reference to the theorizing of Hispanic religious scholars and activists about the Latina/o social location. This omission, coupled with a concentration of African American theorists and religious scholars, reduces oppression to a black-white dichotomy and implies that racism, for Wallis, is having the power to enforce racial prejudices. Because power lies in the hands of whites, Wallis claims that "white racism is primarily a white responsibility," insisting that "there is no such thing as black racism."[26] However, such a definition is problematic for a number of reasons. First, how do we define racism when the president, probably the most powerful person on earth, is black? Second, how do we understand racism when a portion of the Hispanic population is white? Third, when these comments are reprinted twenty years later in 2007, Wallis offers no theoretical update on the concept of racism, nor does he include other groups that are discriminated against but are not black.[27] And fourth, most importantly, if whites created racism, and only whites can solve this problem, then what role do the minoritized play in creating a new social order? There is no need for blacks, let alone Latina/os, to be part of the process. In his opposition to racism, Wallis dismisses minoritized opposition to his understanding of racism and how to fix it.

Wallis' magazine, first published in 1971, does an excellent job of including perspectives and issues crucial to the African American community that whites must consider. Almost every issue since its inception deals with the African American perspective or includes a feature article by a renowned black scholar (most notably Vincent Harding and James Cone). Until around 2006, however, the magazine seldom considered the Hispanic voice, Latino/a issues, or the inclusion of prominent Hispanic religious scholars and activists.

Starting in the summer of 1976, Wallis' magazine did begin the exploration of the Latin American social location, publishing the first Latin American voice (Dom Helder Camara).[28] Since then, *Sojourners* has returned to Latin American concerns and struggles a multitude of times, attempting to include the voices of many Latin American thinkers and activists, especially during the 1980s, when many editions were dedicated to the U.S.-backed Central American wars. It should be noted that Wallis' and the magazine's analysis of the Latin American liberationist movement is sophisticated and clearly places both him and his magazine as allies in the struggle against U.S. hegemony.

Nevertheless, Wallis, along with Sider and Campolo, falls into the error, common among Euroamericans, of confusing the Latin American social location with the U.S. Hispanic social location. While the two are naturally similar in some ways (e.g., language), they are also radically different, operating under different structures of oppression. To look to Latin Americans to be the voice of U.S. Hispanics is to contribute to the continuing invisibility of the latter. And while it is true that a topic of concern to U.S. Hispanics (the United Farm Workers) was first dealt with in an article in the May 1975 issue of *PostAmerican*,[29] followed in 1977 by an entire issue on the United Farm Workers, including an interview with César Chávez,[30] Latina/os remained the object rather than the subject of the conversation. After that 1977 issue, it would be five years before Hispanics' concerns or voices would again be explored in an article, and nineteen years before an entire issue would focus on a Hispanic-centric concern.[31] When we consider how many issues dealt with poverty, oppression, and marginalization, the absence of Hispanics is troubling.

In 1984 *Sojourners* nearly spent more time on Hispanic issues than in the previous thirteen years combined.[32] But even though an entire edition in 1985 and another in 1986 were dedicated to the 1980s Sanctuary Movement, the topic dealt more with Latin America than with U.S. Hispanics, as evidenced by the lack of Latino/a voices in either issue. Since 1986, Latino/a concerns have made sporadic appearances, and when they have, the articles have mainly focused on immigration, as if no other concerns faced Hispanics. Where are the articles about English-only ordinances, liberative-based activities of groups like the Young Lords, discrimination and abuse against Latino/as by police, poverty, housing conditions, and dilapidated schools in the *barrios*. It is not until December 1988, that a book written by a Latina/o on issues dealing with the Hispanic social location is reviewed.[33] The first time a Hispanic is included in a forum article, in which different people write on one issue, is in the November 1989 issue.[34] By the 1990s, the word "Latino" begins to appear routinely in articles dealing with issues of oppression, even though the group still remains the object, not subject, of the discussion and the focus remains on a black-white dichotomy.[35] The first time that a Hispanic writes a feature article on a Latina/o issue is in August 1992.[36] That same year Aaron Gallegos, a sixth-generation Californian, begins writing articles for the magazine, many of which have a Hispanic focus. Thanks to his articles, the Hispanic perspective begins to be included regularly twenty-one years after the founding of the magazine. But by the new millennium it appeares that the Hispanic voice is again submerged, with few articles written by Latino/as about Hispanic issues, let alone articles about Hispanics. The few that appear are mainly relegated to the culture section. It would be nineteen years from the 1977 issue dealing with the United Farm Workers before an entire issue again deals with the Latino/a social location. The cover of the July 2006 issue shows a Hispanic couple next to the caption "We Are America: An Immigrant's Story." In September 2007, the magazine focuss on the New Sanctuary Movement. And the following April, the focus is on the Latino/a pentecostal movement. While Hispanics have started appearing in *Sojourners*, still little or no attention has been given to their contribution to the religious discourse. They remain mainly the object of discourse.

CONCLUSION

Understanding the failure of Euroamerican ethicists or of religious activists from the Religious Right, Center, or Left to recognize Hispanic contributions to religious discourse is important in understanding why Latino/as should move beyond Eurocentric ethics and activism. We should be cautious about adopting their methodologies or worldviews, because they have rejected us by not seriously engaging us in discourse, refusing to consider the contributions our scholarship can make. They reject us by ignoring our social location. They reject us by speaking for us. They reject us when they refuse to welcome us (except for a token Hispanic face here and there) at the conference table where praxes are formulated. It is not so much that Hispanics need to reject Eurocentric ethics; it is that we have never been a true partner in the conversation. Maybe what the first two chapters of this book are doing is simply recognizing the status quo, that all present lines of communication are one way, from Euroamerican religious ethicists and activists toward Hispanics. If communication cannot be two way, then why do we continue to insist?

Please note: I am not begging that the voices and scholarship of Hispanics be explored by the Euroamerican center. If its consciousness has yet to be raised to an awareness of contributions Hispanics can make to the discourse, then insisting on including these marginalized voices remains a futile exercise. It remains the prerogative of any scholar or religious activist to choose who will or will not influence his or her construction of reality. Meanwhile, a Hispanic-centric ethics stands ready to work and cooperate with anyone from the Religious Right, Center, or Left who accepts Latino/as as partners in *la lucha para la liberación*.

Latino/a ethical thought rejects Eurocentric ethical frameworks not because they are Eurocentric, but because (1) they are co-opted by the social and political forces of empire in which they are embedded, and (2) their refusal to include the Latina/o voice in the discourse makes it impossible for them to understand liberative ethics at all. What we must reject is any ethical framework or analysis that either insists on speaking for the marginalized while refusing to understand our social location or, worse, paternalistically believes that its so-called universal truths or worldview construction automatically includes us. Failure to move beyond Eurocentric ethics reduces Hispanics and their concerns to a pawn within the overall U.S. cultural wars, in which each side strives for the title of supreme moral voice of the United States.

Because the Religious Right, Center, and Left remain complicit with empire, they fail to provide Hispanics with a moral framework from which to construct praxis that can lead to full liberation and salvation. On what foundation, then, can Hispanics base their moral agency? To point out the deficiency of Euroamerican ethics is neither to question the sincerity and goodwill of Christians on both sides of the U.S. cultural wars nor to discredit their attempt to follow the teachings of Jesus Christ faithfully as they understand those teachings. The ethics emanating from the Religious Right, Center, and Left are deficient because the social location of those constructing such ethics is embedded in an empire detrimental to Latino/as (and other marginalized groups). These three Euroamerican groups remain a product of an empire that taught them a status quo and taught them to see it as normal and legitimate, blinding them to their complicity with structures pregnant with institutional violence. Since they are unable even to recognize their own complicity with empire, their voice, no matter how "liberating" it may sound, is antithesis to the liberative ethics Hispanics struggle to achieve. For this reason, our salvation will not be found in a Euroamerican religious conservative or liberal approach to social issues affecting us. Our liberation will be discovered only when we begin to construct our own ethical and moral foundation rooted within our social location and using our cultural symbols. It is to this task that the rest of this book turns its attention.

II

RECONSTRUCTING ETHICS

3   WHERE WE HAVE BEEN

In the first section of the book we explored Eurocentric ethics and found little or no room for the Hispanic voice. In this section we look at our own scholarship, customs, and traditions as a foundation upon which to construct an indigenous framework from which to conduct moral reasoning. We begin by recognizing that surveys of the different disciplines within religious studies reveal the field of Christian ethics was, and continues to be, the one in which Hispanics are most underrepresented. Yet ironically, almost every Latina/o religious scholar seems to be preoccupied with a moral response to social issues, focusing on liberation from oppressive structures. At the start of the new millennium, the number of Latina/os who were actively involved in the discipline of Christian ethics, as recognized and defined by the Society of Christian Ethics, could be counted on one hand. They were (in order of obtaining their doctorate) Ismael García,[1] Eldin Villafañe,[2] Ada María Isasi-Díaz,[3] Michael Manuel Mendiola,[4] and I.[5] Most Hispanics who obtained a doctorate in religious studies seemed to concentrate on biblical studies, theology, or religious history. The uninformed observer could easily conclude that Hispanic scholars are neither interested in the field of ethics nor engaged in the scholarly pursuit of moral reasoning. Such a conclusion would be an error.

There are several reasons why more Hispanics have not pursued doctorates in ethics—from blatant ethnic discrimination within the field to a worldview and methodology incongruent with a Latina/o milieu. Probably the underlying reason is how Euroamericans have come to define the field. The question is not whether Hispanic scholars participate in the discipline of ethics, but whether Euroamerican scholars are aware of that participation, for the dominant academic culture's categorizing of educational disciplines is generally counter-intuitive to the more holistic and multidisciplinary approach Hispanics employ in their scholarship. When Hispanic religious studies first began to develop in the 1970s, Latina/o scholars in all disciplines emphasized the need to challenge oppressive structures in society, the church, and the academy. Nearly all scholarship conducted by Latino/a religious scholars, regardless of their focus of expertise, had a liberative, praxis-oriented component. For example, Justo González (a historian) has written a multitude of books that explore ethical responses to theological positions detrimental to Hispanics;[6] María Pilar Aquino (a theologian) explores a theological response to the oppression of Latinas;[7] and Virgilio Elizondo (a pastoral theologian) has written a groundbreaking book providing an ethical response to Mexican Americans' oppression based on their social location of *mestizaje.*[8] For many early Hispanic religious scholars, the purpose of scholarship was to bring relief, hope, salvation, and liberation to their disenfranchised communities.

Even though many Latina/o religious scholars became theologians, hermeneutics scholars, and historians, most were scholar-activists concerned with bringing change to what they perceived to be oppressive social and ecclesiastic structures.[9] Whatever their fields of specialization or expertise, they were eager to develop subversive praxis to respond to the moral dilemmas faced by Hispanics. In a very real sense, they were all ethicists—not official ethicists recognizable by the Society of Christian Ethics, but ethicists all the same. Why? Because there is an inseparable bond between the act of bringing about a more just and moral existence for Latina/os and the different disciplines that study religion. Hispanic religious thought, to be Latino/a, bases itself on a commitment to justice that serves as a critical reflection of the lived experiences of disenfranchised *comunidades* emboldened in the struggle for social change. This scholarship stems from a need to articulate liberative responses to moral dilemmas faced by Hispanic communities, responses that would contribute significantly to bringing about justice.

We can say first and foremost, and most Latina/os would agree, that all religious thought, including moral reasoning, is contextual. For any Hispanic-based ethics to be relevant it must reflect the social location of the Latina/o community, specifically its faith and practices. Since the start several decades ago of Latina/o-based religious scholarly thought, it has been a liberative-driven discourse contextualized on what it means to be part of a Hispanic faith community. But contexts are always in flux. The world faced by Hispanics in the last millennium is quite different from the world they face today. While oppressive structures remain, they are better masked in a politically correct milieu, and manifested differently.

The present generation of Hispanic scholars of religion is recontextualizing its interpretive framework in light of its present circumstances. To this end it is exploring recent developments in the study of Latino/a religions. It is important to recognize here the recent increase in junior scholars and Ph.D. candidates in the field. As already mentioned, the new millennium began with only five Christian ethicists holding doctoral degrees. In 2010, about a dozen are active, most of them graduate students. Many reasons can be given for this development, including the creation of a Latino/a Working Group within the Society of Christian Ethics. What is important for our purposes is that Hispanic Ph.D. graduate students are consciously deciding to specialize in ethics. Ten years into the new millennium, a discipline that can be called Hispanic ethics is developing, not yet fully formed, but rooted in forty years of Hispanic religious scholarship.

What this means is that scholars cannot yet draw on an extensive body of literature written by Hispanic ethicists dealing specifically with the discipline of Latina/o ethics. With the exception of a few books,[10] there is little upon which to formulate an indigenous methodology of conducting Hispanic ethical analysis.[11] There is a danger, in such a situation, that the voice of a particular Hispanic scholar will be elevated as the ultimate source of ethical knowledge; it was for such an elevation of Euroamerican male ethicists that I critiqued the dominant academic culture in the first chapter. To counter this risk, we must explore how ethical thought is constructed within the Hispanic *comunidad*. To that end, in this chapter we will review the foundational Latina/o religious scholarship on which a Hispanic ethics can be constructed.

This new subfield, called Latina/o Christian ethics, though presently worked in by few, still represents significant diversity of thought. Some scholars practicing in this field, especially those among the newer generation of ethicists, still base their moral reasoning on Eurocentric ethical thought. Others, myself included, are more suspicious of Eurocentric ethical frameworks, which are blind to their complicity with the prevailing oppressive social structures. Regardless of the diversity in thought and methodology among Hispanic ethicists, their different styles of moral reasoning still appear to be bound together by a cultural distinctness formed through collective experiences and memories of alienation and injustices. Though we must avoid essentializing Hispanic ethics as if it had a single monolithic paradigm, we can still affirm that certain common and widely shared experiences and memories shape the Latino/a existential being and dominate Hispanic moral discourse. Our responses to a collective memory of systematic abuse can help explain this emerging Latina/o ethics—an ethics developed from a more general Hispanic religious scholarship. It is to some of these characteristics of Latina/o religious scholarship that we now turn.

AN ETHICS *EN LO COTIDIANO*

Among the most important concepts in Latina/o ethical analysis is *lo cotidiano*,[12] which can be understood as the everyday along with all of its particularities. As such, it can provide an interpretive lens by which the Latina/o reality can be understood. María Pilar Aquino reminds us that

> [d]aily relationships become the basis and image of all social relations. This is why analysts stress that daily life permeates the public as well as the private spheres, because the activities carried out in both spheres "imply a level of dailiness, daily actions that confer upon this oppression, day after day, an air of naturalness." This is why women stress the need to change the way things are done in daily life in order to construct equal models of interhuman relationships. (1993: 40)

To focus on the daily existence of Latina/os is to analyze critically the good and bad that shape and form the daily life of a Hispanic. The study of *lo cotidiano*, therefore, has the potential to take us beyond analysis, becoming both the catalyst for structural changes and a foundation upon which all liberative ethical praxis is determined and implemented.

One of Hispanics' main critiques of the way Euroamericans do ethical analysis is that they tend to center the discourse on the abstract, if not the aesthetic. Case studies are created not as a guide for participating in community-changing praxis, but to test ethical concepts and analytically push the limits of moral reasoning. At the start of the twentieth century, many Eurocentric ethicists focused their discussion upon implementing praxis to deal with particular ethical dilemmas. Unfortunately, since then the emphasis of ethical discourse has shifted to understanding the nature of ethics, specifically questions concerning what are virtues and what is the good. But for ethical discourse to be relevant for Hispanics, ethics must be contextualized in *lo cotidiano*. Christian Latino/as recognize that the God they worship became human, enfleshing Godself, then and now, in the everyday lives and experiences of the dispossessed. Hispanics experience the salvific nature of God in the daily struggles to be recognized as fully human. God's presence and accompaniment in the everyday struggle for social justice makes whatever occurs in the daily life of Latina/os the subject and source for all Hispanic ethical reflection.

Lo cotidiano incorporates the hermeneutics of the self, usually seen as unscholarly by Eurocentric ethicists. Even so, Hispanic religious scholars constantly and consistently employ *lo cotidiano* in order to collapse the dichotomy between theory and praxis. Thus Hispanic ethical analysis is able to avoid lifeless ethical understandings of moral dilemmas. The inclusion of Latino/a everyday struggles provides such analysis with a heart that counters the Eurocentric tendency to overemphasize the rational. Any ethical framework that is to be indigenous to the Hispanic community must therefore be unapologetically anchored in the autobiographical stories and testimonies of the disenfranchised. It must begin with *lo cotidiano* as experienced and understood by the marginalized Latina/o communities. The testimonies of attempting to survive as an undocumented immigrant, as a physically and/or sexually abused spouse, as a laborer relegated to the most demeaning and menial employment, or as a second-class citizen who everyday is reminded she or he doesn't belong become the bases on which God is understood, God's presence is experienced, and God's will for justice is implemented.

The trials and tribulations of Hispanics struggling for their humanity and dignity become the starting point for any type of indigenous Latino/a ethical framework. As can be expected, this approach will challenge the privileged position occupied at the top of religious hierarchies, where Euroamerican moral agents have historically insisted on being the sole legitimate interpreters of what is and what is not moral. Ethics for Hispanics can be done only with one's feet firmly planted on the concrete sidewalks of the *barrios*, the dirt roads of the migrant trails, the rich soil of the farms, or any-where else Latina/os find themselves struggling against oppressive structures. To ground Hispanic ethical reasoning in *lo cotidiano* is to subvert the normalized direction of the discourse, which is from the center toward the periphery. The study of the everyday brings the margins to the center, and in the process challenges those accus-tomed to setting the parameters of ethical discourse.

For Hispanics, the primary source for doing ethics is their lived, everyday experience. It is *lo cotidiano* that provides Latina/os with an "epistemological privilege." Latino/as know how to live and sur-vive in both the center and the periphery of society, unlike those privileged by the prevailing social structures, which generally fail to understand the marginalized experience. Yet ironically, making *lo cotidiano* the privileged source or *locus theologicus* of Latina/os con-flicts with how Euroamericans have legitimized ethical discourse. Many within the dominant culture dismiss the identity or social location of the one attempting to determine ethical responses, because in their minds, the inclusion of the personal compromises a so-called objective reading of the ethical dilemma faced. Never-theless, Latino/as reject the Eurocentric ethical methodology that requires the detachment of the moral agent doing the analysis as a means of ensuring autonomy. Most Hispanic ethicists would argue that one cannot deliberate on moral questions with any integrity without an intimate understanding of the dilemma faced. And if a scholar tries to deliberate on such matters from a position of detachment, her or his ability to comprehend fully the complexity of any moral dilemma will be seriously compromised. Simply stated, any ethical framework not rooted in the everyday of the marginal-ized is of no use to Latina/os.

AN ETHICS *DE NEPANTLA*

Lo cotidiano recognizes that ethics is conducted with a preferential option for those living on the hyphen in *Hispanic-American*. This preferential option does not include all who claim "Latinoness" but is reserved for Hispanics who are poor, that is, the culturally oppressed and socially dispossessed, those forced to live on the bor-ders of reality. It is from the discursive space of the borders that Hispanics must do most of their ethical analysis.

When we think of borders, we usually think of the 1,833-mile line that separated the United States from the rest of Latin America that was created in the 1830s, a line created by a superior U.S. military. To Latino/as this demarcation is known—and rightly so—as the scar caused by the First and Third World rubbing up against each other. Geographically, it makes sense to consider the region surrounding this artificial line, where 13 million Americans and Mexicans reside, as the borderlands. But borderlands are more than just a geographical reality—they symbolize the existential reality of all U.S. Latina/os. Regardless of where Hispanics live, how long they have lived there, or how they or their ancestors came to find themselves in the United States, they all live on the borders. They need not physically live close to the line separating the U.S. from their countries of origin. Wherever Hispanics live, there are borders between them and Euroamericans. Invisible borders in Seattle, Washington; Fargo, North Dakota; Sioux City, Iowa; and Jackson, Mississippi are just as real as the physical borders of Chula Vista, California; Douglas, Arizona; and El Paso, Texas. To be a Hispanic living anywhere in the U.S. is to live constantly on the border, that is, the borders between power and disenfranchisement, between privilege and dispossession, between whiteness and "color." Most U.S. Hispanics, regardless of where they physically live, live on the borderlands; and it is from this social location that any ethical analysis that is to be called Hispanic-based must originate.

On these borders exists one of the major motifs influencing Hispanic moral reasoning, the experience of victimization. The borders are where the brokenness of Hispanic lives is more evident. Latina/os living on the borders in the United States are disjointed from the culture of their heritage and the culture in which they reside, outsiders and foreigners to both. In this in-between place of borders, Latina/os confront economic exploitation and political marginalization. All too often, their identity is reduced by the dominant culture to paternalistically inspired caricatures. Not surprisingly, in response, almost all religious scholarship by Hispanics focuses on social ethics, deeply rooted in the quest for justice. Regardless of whether the religious scholar is an ethicist or not, her or his scholarship is highly influenced by the task of bringing a more just reality to social issues confronting the Latina/o *comunidad*.

The *comunidad*'s middle ground, which is located on the borders, is what Hispanics have come to call their *nepantla* location.[13] The term originates among the indigenous contributions to the overall *Latinidad*. Coined by one of the indigenous roots of Hispanics, the Aztecs, the word connotes being in the middle, "that situation," as J. Jorge Klor de Alva reminds us, "in which a person remains suspended in the middle between a lost or disfigured past and a present that has not been assimilated or understood" (1982: 353). To be in the middle means denying neither the indigenous customs and traditions of Hispanics nor the new religions and concepts brought about by the vicissitudes of conflicting cultures. The Latina/o *mestizaje*, that is, the cultural, political, religious, social, and physical "mixing" birthed from the pain and anguish of continuous conquest, contributes to a notion of *nepantla* that describes the recognition that within most Latino/as' veins flows the blood of both the conquerors and the conquered. From the *nepantla* social location of being in the middle, or on the border, any ethical analysis that is to be called Hispanic must originate with the goal of seeking justice-based alternatives to the struggles of *lo cotidiano* for communal survival.

AN ETHICS *PARA LA LUCHA*

As a child, I remember my parents' response every time they were asked, "*¿cómo está?*" "*Ahí,*" they would respond, "*en la lucha.*" When they responded to the question, how were they doing, by saying they were *en la lucha*, translated as "in the struggle" or "in the fight," they were commenting on the existential reality of *lo cotidiano*. To be in *nepantla*, living on the borders between marginality and acceptance, is to struggle for your family's daily bread, to fight for your family's basic human dignity. Even those minor privileges taken for granted by the dominant culture (e.g., not having to be reminded every single day of one's ethnicity) are a constant *lucha* for Hispanics.[14] According to Ada María Isasi-Díaz, speaking specifically about Latinas (and I would add Latinos),

> An anthropology developed out of the lived-experience of Latinas centers on a subject who struggles to survive and who understands herself as one who struggles. . . . Of course the centrality of struggle as a constitutive element of the everyday lives of Latinas, of Latinas' self-construction, can be understood and grasped only against a background of oppression due to specific historical injustices that are the cause of great suffering. But in listening carefully to grassroot Latinas, one finds that what locates us in life is not suffering but *la lucha* to survive. To consider suffering as what locates us would mean that we understand ourselves not as a moral subject but as one acted upon by the oppressors. (1993: 168)

La lucha for survival not only describes the Hispanic social location; it also provides the means by which Latina/os develop their world-view, learn to maneuver among the consequences of ethnic discrimination, and begin to construct a more liberative understanding of themselves. To discover a more accurate understanding of the Hispanic social location is to recognize that it may be possible to change that reality. Change to what? To the promise given by Christ that signified his mission: "I came that they may have life, and have it abundantly" (John 10:10). The goal of liberative ethics, in a nutshell, is for all of humanity, including Latino/as, to experience the fullness of life as willed by the God of life.

Latino/a ethics emphasizes a contextual approach to changing reality. This is contrary to a normative Eurocentric ethics that fails critically to deal with power and how it works and thus leads scholars to base their abstract ethical reasoning on a naïve optimism. But regardless of how sophisticated or complex is the manner in which Eurocentric ethics is constructed, *la lucha*, the struggle and needs of the marginalized, takes precedence. Because it is easier for a camel to go through the eye of a needle than for the beneficiaries of the present social structures to be convinced, converted, or cajoled into freely and willingly abdicating the ethics that secures their privileged position, *la lucha* becomes a struggle toward a revolutionary restructuring of how power is presently distributed and how knowledge is constructed. But such a praxis cannot come to be unless Hispanic consciousness is first raised so that Hispanics understand who they are and why, in spite of their best efforts, they remain disenfranchised.

This daily *lucha* for survival causes any ethical Latina/o reflection to stress and emphasize identity—an identity shaped by a history of cultural, political, and economic conquest and subjugation. This self-definition is never individualistic, but a communal endeavor, a self-understanding of a people—a people struggling to survive. Not surprisingly, any Latina/o ethics formulated in an environment so hostile toward Hispanics creates a response focused on constructing a communal identity capable of leading Latina/os toward a new self-understanding ripe with dignity and a praxis that could lead *la comunidad* toward self-determination. For Latina ethicist Isasi-Díaz, who is probably more responsible than any other person for developing this ethical concept, this ethics based on the struggle to survive is multifaceted. Not only must Latinas face sexism from their *hermanos* within *la comunidad*, they must also face ethnic discrimination from their Euroamerican sisters within the feminist movement. Latina/os must face multifaceted manifestations of oppression not alone but as *la comunidad*, acting *en conjunto*, that is, in conjunction with each other.

AN ETHICS *EN CONJUNTO*

It is crucial to note that *la lucha* for survival is not an individual quest. For Latina/os, it is never the individual's betterment that takes priority, but the sustainability of the Hispanic community and the quality of life it lives. Contrary to the salient individualistic motif among Euroamericans, Hispanic religious thought attempts to be communal. According to José David Rodríguez and Loida I. Martell-Otero,

> This particular [communal] method of doing theology is very characteristic of Hispanic American theology and is what we call in Spanish *teología en conjunto*. Literally, *en conjunto* means "in conjunction," or "conjoined in," implying not only the coming together but also the integration and intimacy involved in such sharing. It is reminiscent of the human body, whose various joints, tendons, muscles, and bones must be conjoined in order for it to function in an adequate way. Thus, we use the term *teología en conjunto* to emphasize two fundamental aspects affecting Hispanic theology: its rich diversity and its integral collaborative spirit. (1997: 1)[15]

Like theology, moral reasoning is conducted within, by, and for the overall *comunidad*. Multifarious Latina/o voices are bound by a holistic collaborative spirit that emerges when the faith community gathers to share the Word of God, their stories of suffering, and their pilgrimage through artificial borders. To be in community reveals how the damage inflicted for being Hispanic is compounded on the social, psychological, spiritual, physiological, emotional, and financial levels of existence, as well as across generations.[16]

Ethics *en conjunto*, as a collaborative methodology, is privileged by Hispanic ethicists over abstract ethical theories generated from the safety of ivory towers because it attempts to understand faith and vocation as contextualized in the lives and struggles of Latino/as. This strategy calls for the full participation of every level of the community. The goal of an ethics *en conjunto* is for the marginalized community to (1) analyze the reality of *lo cotidiano*, (2) reflect on what the good news of the biblical text has to say about this reality, (3) implement praxis that can bring about a more just society, and (4) reflect on the results of this praxis to ascertain if new actions are required.

For Hispanics, true ethical analysis relies on multiple Latina/o voices responding from a *nepantla* space to *la lucha* of *lo cotidiano* in light of the Christian faith of *la comunidad*. Such an approach questions the way of conducting ethics that has been made normative by the dominant culture. Because moral reasoning *en conjunto* requires a conversation, it must be grounded in the Hispanic *comunidad*. This keeps ethical analysis real and practical, because it focuses on the struggle against the dehumanization and disenfranchisement of Latina/os. Additionally, normalized authoritative ethical paradigms of the dominant culture are unmasked as Hispanic voices from "the underside" assert themselves in the general colloquy. The communal recovery of Christianity in moral reasoning creates an ethics from, by, and for Hispanics that remains resistant to the injustices faced by *la comunidad*.

Hispanic ethicists cannot stand aloof from *la comunidad* but must be organic intellectuals, part of the community, sharing in *lo cotidiano*. These ethicists stand side by side with the marginalized, accompanying them in their struggles while engaging in moral reasoning. This incarnational approach to ethics is based on the Gospel of John's witness that the Word "dwelled among us" (1:14). Such an ethics becomes autobiographical, because ethicists cease to speak about oppressed Latino/as as if they were objects of scholastic study, and instead employ the term "we."

AN ETHICS *DE ACOMPAÑAMIENTO*

The communal methodology employed in Hispanic ethical reasoning ensures that no Latino/a stands alone to face the overwhelming oppressive structures designed to rob them of their personhood and dignity. In effect, the praxis of *acompañamiento*, of accompanying, is how Latino/as make a preferential option for the oppressed.[17] It is a praxis of being present alongside disenfranchised Latina/o *comunidades* in *lo cotidiano* and in *la lucha*. This option of everyday presence becomes an ethics that emphasizes the term "we," an ethics *de acompañamiento* in *la lucha*, based on the concept of God taking on flesh to accompany God's people in their struggle. Being befriended

by God restores to the so-called nonpersons of history their humanity, worth, and dignity. According to Roberto Goizueta,

> The preferential option for the poor thus implies a preferential
> option for the home, the city, and, the crossroads where home and
> city meet, the church. Because it is an option for particular flesh-
> and-blood persons, it will also be an option for particular *places*,
> the places where the poor live, die, and struggle for survival. To
> "opt for the poor" is thus to place ourselves *there*, to *accompany*
> the poor person in his or her life, death, and struggle for survival.
> A U.S. Hispanic theology will thus be preferentially (again, not
> exclusively) *a domestic, urban theology of accompaniment*. Such
> a theology would, in turn, underscore three dimensions of the
> option for the poor: 1) the affective dimension, as enfleshed in
> particular relationships; 2) the spatial, geographical dimension, as
> represented by the unity of home and city; 3) the dimension of
> interiority, as reflected in the theologian's own, personal appropri-
> ation of the option for the poor; and 4) the spiritual dimension, as
> incarnated in the faith of the poor, which transgresses all spatial,
> geographic barriers. (1995: 192; emphasis in original)

Even the incarnated God, as Jesus, is not alone, for those who are
to be disciples accompany Jesus on his way to the cross during *his*
struggle. The historical act is repeated each year throughout many
barrios on Good Friday. In an event known as *Via Crucis, la comunidad* gathers for a reenactment of the passion narrative, to walk
with Jesus on his way to Calvary. This act of solidarity reaffirms the
community's bond with a God who suffers and struggles alongside
them. In spite of the hopelessness of Good Friday, this bond serves
as a glimmer of a possible resurrected hope that can become the
strength to continue *la lucha*, and, dare we say it, a hope of bringing change to the overarching structures that cause death. To do
ethics is to be *acompañado* by Jesus and, in turn, to imitate Jesus
by accompanying our neighbors, specifically our neighbors who are
disenfranchised. In this fashion, Latino/a-based ethics looks toward
Jesus as the revealer of moral agency. The Jesus narrative serves as
both the basic criterion of God's revelation and the basis for ethical
reasoning and future praxis.

A CHRISTOCENTRIC ETHICS

For Christian Latina/o ethics to be Christian and Hispanic, it must be Christocentric.[18] Without Christ it can still be a Hispanic ethics, but it cannot be Christian. The theological question, who is Christ? is inseparable from the ethical question, what are we to do? But before considering praxis, Latina/os must first determine on which Christ they will anchor their moral reasoning on. Is it the Christ constructed by Euroamericans? Well-meaning Euroamericans, both conservative and liberal, insist that the true Christ is the one they have created in their image. This is problematic, because any construction of Christ is the collective representation of a certain group of people, a symbolic expression that helps that group solidify as a faith community, providing them with a sense of unity. Such a Christ transmits how their culture defines morality to the next generation, in effect providing divine sanction for how the culture organizes itself and determines which social behaviors to uphold. The question Latino/as must ask themselves is whether the Jesus of the dominant Euroamerican culture is the same Christ who can provide Hispanics with a foundation upon which to conduct moral reasoning.

The Euroamerican Christ has historically been used (or muted) to divinely justify societal actions that have contributed to the marginalization of Hispanics. The Euroamerican Jesus is the Christ who inspired the quasireligious ideology of Manifest Destiny, which led the United States in the military conquest of northern Mexico, preventing that nation from building wealth, and disenfranchising those over whom the border crossed. The Euroamerican Jesus is the Christ who remained silent during the implementation of gunboat diplomacy that denied Latin American nations their sovereignty and provided U.S. corporations freedom and protection while they extracted the cheap labor and natural resources of a people. The Euroamerican Jesus is the Christ of present-day presidents and politicians whose main purpose is the maintenance of U.S. global hegemony. This domination of nonwhites abroad is mirrored domestically in the disproportionate disenfranchisement of Hispanics from the economic and political benefits of society. In short, Latina/os should remain leery of the Euroamerican Christ because of his complicity with empire.

Versions of Christ presented to Hispanics by well-meaning Euroamerican scholars and clergy can be used to impose an identity on Latina/os. Used in this way, these Euroamerican Christs can then be misconstrued as the intellectual and/or spiritual saviors of Hispanics. It should not be surprising that many Latino/as look toward Eurocentric scholarship and doctrines in order to revitalize their study and understanding of Christ. But to do so causes Hispanics to envision Christ as a cultural extension of the Eurocentric mission. The necessary process of formulating their own Hispanic space from which they can commune with a Christ indigenous to their own social location begins with the realization that Eurocentric thought has historically been hostile to the existential being of Latina/os.

It really does not matter how progressively Euroamericans construct Jesus or how liberally they attempt to interpret his words. As long as Latino/as bend their knees to a Christ who is silent about what it means to live at the margins of Euroamerican power and privilege, as long as this Christ refuses to motivate action among Euroamerican churches to speak out about the marginalization faced throughout the *barrios* of this nation, as long as this Christ does not draw Euroamericans out to stand in solidarity with the thousands who die in the Sonoran desert of Arizona because of unjust immigration laws, those Hispanics who insist on worshipping the Christ who looks and acts like the dominant culture will in fact be worshipping the symbolic cause of their oppression. This is more than simply following a Jesus who looks Hispanic (whatever looking Hispanic means). Hispanic moral reasoning insists on basing its ethical analysis on a Christ *en acompañamiento* with Hispanics and thus has something important to say to the marginalized, a message indecipherable to those accustomed to their power and privilege.

In order to sever the link between power and disenfranchisement, between privilege and marginality, Christ must be recognized as ontologically Hispanic. Just as Euroamericans have for centuries worshipped a Christ in their own image, it becomes significant for Latina/os to see the deity as an ethnic Hispanic. Why? Because the white Christ of Euroamerican history has been the Christ who justified the historical reality of colonialism, slavery, racism, and oppression. It was in the name of this white Christ, the Christ who symbolized the protection of white Christian civilization from so-called Hispanic inferiority, that the marginalization of Hispanics became normalized and legitimized in the eyes of white America.

The pervasiveness of the white Euroamerican Christ can be noted in the colonization of the minds of Hispanics who have been taught to bend their knees not only to the image of this Euroamerican Christ but also to the religiosity that that image signifies—a religiosity detrimental to the Latina/o existence.

Nevertheless, the Latina/o Christ is informed by the historical identification of Jesus with those who suffer under oppression. Christ's "Latinoness" is not due to some simplistic attempt to be politically correct, nor to some psychological need of Latina/os to see a deity through their own cultural signs. Jesus is Hispanic because the biblical witness of God is of one who takes sides with the least among us against those who oppress them. In an America founded on racism and ethnic discrimination, Hispanics (along with other communities of color) were the ones being oppressed, the ones who were hungry, thirsty, cast out, naked, afflicted, and incarcerated.[19]

Consequently, only a Latina/o Christ can liberate Hispanics. Why? Because Eurocentric Christs, no matter how benignly they are presented, will always be incongruent with the disenfranchised reality Latino/as are forced to occupy. The question Latino/as must ask themselves is, does the Euroamerican Christ provide life and provide it abundantly for Hispanics (John 10:10)? If history is any guide, the Euroamerican Christ and/or his church has mostly provided disenfranchisement, despair, and death. In short, salvation for Hispanics will not be found in the divine symbols of the Euroamerican culture. To commune with a Hispanic Christ is to incarnate the gospel message within the marginalized spaces of the *barrios* so that the actions and words of Jesus can infuse *la comunidad* with the hope of survival and liberation. For this reason, the Euroamerican Christ, who has served as the Hispanic anti-Christ, needs to be rejected for a Christ constructed from within the Latino/a ethos.[20]

It is not enough to insist that a Euroamerican Christ needs to be rejected. We must also envision how Christ is incarnated in the historical social location of Latina/os. We begin by realizing that whatever Christ means to Hispanics, he must be understood within sociohistorical and eco-political contexts of the Latina/o community of faith that is responding to the biblical message of liberation. For Latina/os, however, Christ is defined or understood foremost as a liberator. But Christ as liberator moves beyond narrow constructs of liberating Latino/as from "personal sins." The Christ of Hispanics is just as concerned with the sins of the entire community, specifically of those within the dominant culture, whose sins wreak chaos and havoc upon the lives of those forced to reside on the margins. From the underside of U.S. culture, where Hispanics are forced to suffer, a quest for a Hispanic Christ becomes a quest for liberation, liberation from racism and ethnic discrimination.

Hispanics are quick to point out that God has historically chosen the least among the people to be agents of God's new creation. It is the stone rejected by the builders that becomes the keystone of God's created order (Matthew 21:42). The biblical story reminds us that it was not Rome, the most powerful city of the known world, where God chose to perform the miracle of the incarnation, nor was it Jerusalem, the center of Yahweh worship; rather, it was impoverished Galilee where God chose first to proclaim the message of the gospels. From the margins of Galilee, the good news goes to the center of religious and political powers—a paradigm that turns the "white man's burden" of Christianizing the margins of whiteness upon its head. Ethical reflections from the perspective of Hispanics identify with a deity who habitually chooses a stone from the margins, rejected by the dominant culture, to carry out God's salvific plan.

The gospel message of liberation from oppressive societal structures resonates with Hispanics who discover that those marginalized in Jesus' time occupied the privileged position of being the first to hear the good news, not because they were holier, nor better people, but because God chooses sides. God makes a preferential option for those who exist under the weight of oppression. The radical nature of the incarnation is not that God became human, but that God assumed the condition of one of *los humildes*, one of the humbled. If God was to reincarnate today, God would come to us in the form of those most despised by the culture, those most humbled. No doubt God would incarnate Godself as an undocumented immigrant, for such immigrants are the ones who are hungry, thirsty, naked, foreign, ill, and, if caught crossing, imprisoned. Why is it important to ground moral reasoning upon an understanding of Christ through the lens of Hispanics? By making those humbled by the dominant culture of Christ's time the recipients of the good news, Jesus emphasized the political edge of his message. Any quest for understanding Christ within the United States requires making marginalized communities of color the starting point of all inquiries. This is not an attempt to romanticize Hispanic marginalization; rather, it is an attempt to understand Christ as a unifying symbol for Latina/os.

A PRAXIS-CENTRIC ETHICS

Ethics is what Jesus did. More important than the narrative of Jesus are his actions. One learns more about God and the biblical text as one "does" more of what Jesus did—feeds the hungry, clothes the naked, attends to the vulnerable. Because oppressive institutions and structures that give rise to colonialism, imperialism, assimilation-ist tendencies, rampant classism, racism, sexism, homophobia, and other such forces are antithetical to the reign of God, and because Jesus' mission was to usher in God's reign, any hope of imitating and continuing the work of Christ must be based upon a confrontational, liberative praxis.[21] Such a praxis is not separate from theory. Euro-centric ethics creates a false dichotomy between thinking or theo-rizing about what is the common good or what is proper virtue and the doing or implementation of actions leading to justice. Hispanic ethical thought collapses the division normatively made between faith and works, doctrine and practice.

Generally speaking, Euroamerican ethicists usually begin with some type of "truth" claim based on some doctrine, biblical passage, church teachings, spiritual revelation, or rational analysis. From this "truth," they determine that an action is required, usually an indi-vidual act of piety. The emphasis is on possessing the "truth," having the right doctrine. However, by relegating action to the individual, they preclude the transformation of the overall power structures. Latina/o moral reasoning repudiates the dominant culture's propo-sition that right doctrine, orthodoxy, takes precedence over right practice, orthopraxis. To do Christian ethics as Hispanics is to move away from an intellectual exercise toward concrete actions that respond to the human condition—a response that is reflective and marked by ethical living.

To do ethics from the Latino/a margins is to attempt to work out truth and theory through reflection and action in solidarity with *la comunidad*. In this sense, praxis is not guided by theory. Ethics done *en conjunto* is not deductive, that is, beginning with some universal truth and determining the appropriate response based on that truth. Hispanics tend to be suspicious of such universal claims, which have a history of justifying Latina/o oppression. In Hispanic ethics, unlike in Eurocentric moral reasoning, theories about a just world and the actions to bring about the transformation of the present unjust world are united. In a very real sense, praxis mediates between Christian ideals concerning God's salvific will for all humans and the actions that are required to bring about God's liberation for humanity.

Not surprisingly, Christian praxis is revolutionary—not in a violent way, but rather on the basis of a faith in a God who so loves all of humanity that God gave us Jesus Christ, who calls his followers to love their neighbors, including their enemies. It is God's will that all of humanity come to salvation, understood as liberation from sin, and not just the individual sin emphasized by Eurocentric ethics, but more importantly, the communal sin manifested in the social structures designed to privilege some at the expense of others. Ethics, as understood by Latina/os, becomes the way by which liberation, or salvation, can be achieved. This is an evangelical praxis that is both a response to Jesus' good news and a calling for Christians, in our case Latino/a Christians, to live out their faith in a here and now situated within a hostile environment. It is a praxis that is both pastoral and prophetic. It is pastoral because its major concern is to provide succor for Hispanics being ground up by the prevailing oppressive structures bent on robbing them of their humanity and dignity. It is prophetic because it provides a vision of a world that could be and engages the prevailing powers to bring about transformative change.

In an earlier book, *Doing Christian Ethics from the Margins*, I argued that the manner in which many Euroamerican Christian ethicists conduct moral reasoning falls short because they argue over abstract moral frameworks rather than *doing* ethics. Many Christians respond in words to the inhuman conditions forced upon the dispossessed when it is much more important to respond in deeds, in actions, in praxis. When a moral Christian life is reduced to individual piety or virtue, it often fails to result in Christian action.

Ethics is action, action that leads to salvation and liberation for both the oppressed and their oppressors. James the brother of Jesus probably said it best:

> My brothers and sisters, where is the gain for someone to say they have faith, if they do nothing? Is faith able to save such a person? If a brother or sister is naked and lacking in daily food, and one of you were to say "Go in peace, be warm and filled," but do not give them what the body needs, where is the gain? Even so, faith without works is dead. Yet someone may say, "You have faith and I have works." Let me see your faith without your works and I will

show you my faith by my works. You believe God is one, and you do well. But even the demons believe and tremble. Do you not see, O foolish one, that faith without works is useless? (James 2:14-20)

Because ethics is fallible, not universal, a "roadmap" leading to Christian action, based on the Roman Catholic social teaching model of seeing, judging, and acting, can be helpful.[22] Using this methodology as foundational for my own moral reasoning, I expanded this model to five basic steps that form a hermeneutical circle (see figure 1 below).

The five-step hermeneutical circle I proposed is as follows: First, observation—the community attempts to understand why the present moral dilemma exists. To observe is to consider seriously the historical situation responsible for the present oppressive circumstances in which Latina/os are forced to live. Understanding the Hispanic social location requires exploring why, how, and when the present oppressive structures were created, maintained, normalized, and legitimized. To observe is consciously to seek the voices of Hispanics who do not inhabit history, voices that are silenced or

FIGURE 1

The Hermeneutical Circle for Ethics

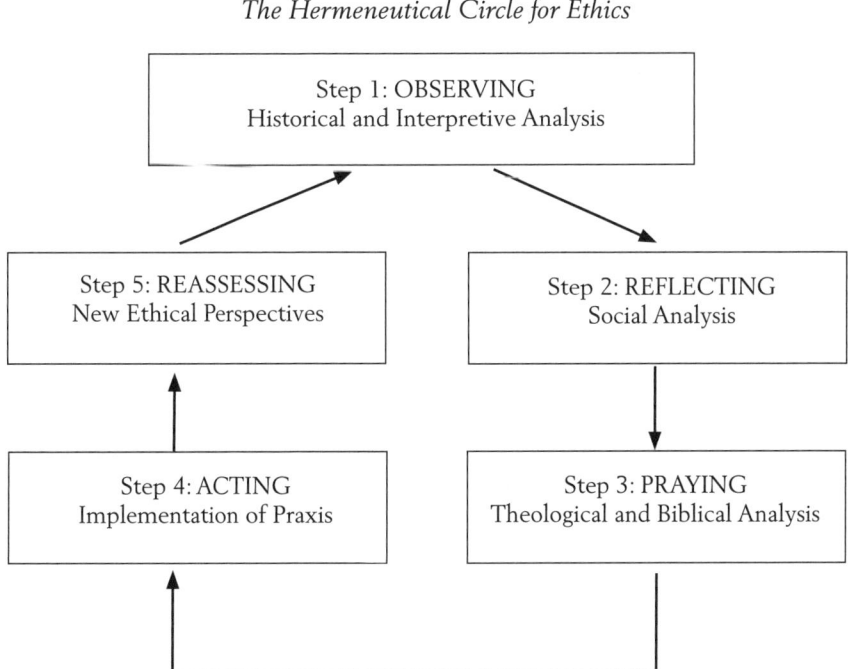

relegated to the margins. It is to attempt to "see" through the eyes of Latino/as who are made poor, who are victimized, and who are made to suffer. To observe is to recover their voices so as to provide a critique to the prevailing powers (2004: 58–61).

Second, reflection—the community attempts to understand how social structures contribute to and maintain the oppression of Latina/os. Society cannot be transformed if it is not first analyzed. The social sciences provide a methodology by which to discern raw data that can elucidate the reality faced by Hispanics. To point out how social mechanisms maintain institutionalized oppression is to point out the sin of the dominant culture. Latino/as cannot respond to oppressive structures adequately unless they fully understand how society has subjugated them economically, socially, and politically and how it maintains its dominance over them (2004: 62–63).

Third, prayer—the community attempts to understand the responsibility of Hispanics of faith. Prayer is not limited to holding a private conversation with the Creator of the universe; prayer is also a communal act by which the members of a Latino/a faith community accompany each other and stand in solidarity during trials and tribulations. Prayer establishes *koinonia*, where Latina/os critically listen to one another's stories and commit to work in solidarity *en la lucha* for full liberation, both spiritually and physically. To pray is to discern God's will by critically applying the biblical text to the moral dilemmas we face. To read the Bible *en conjunto* is to fuse the biblical narrative with *lo cotidiano*, producing a biblical witness capable of addressing the Hispanic *nepantla* (2004: 63–66).

Fourth, action—the community responds to what it claims to believe. Regardless of how sincere and noble Euroamericans may appear to be, theorizing about justice changes nothing. To do ethics as a Latino/a is to do, not simply to theorize. The praxis that is called for moves beyond some paternalistic "charity," to actions geared to dismantle the presiding social structures that are detrimental to Latina/os as well as to all other disenfranchised communities (2004: 66–68).

And finally, reassessment—the community attempts to ensure that the action it took was faithful to the gospel message of liberation and salvation. In this final step, the Latino/a community asks whether the implementation of praxis brought it a greater share of abundant life, and, if so, what additional praxis is required. But if not, the community asks what should be done to replace the previous praxis with new and more effective action. It is by reassessing the effectiveness of the actions taken that Latino/as can gradually create an ethical system. Then, by reflecting upon praxis, they can develop a more correct doctrine, *orthodoxy*. Hence, they turn the Eurocentric model on its head. They repudiate the deductive methodology, according to which the moral agent begins with some truth claim and then moves toward the application of that truth; the Hispanic model thus shatters the subordination of ethics to dogma. It is praxis that forms doctrine, informs the interpretation of Scripture, and shapes the system of ethics (2004: 68–69).

MOVING BEYOND HISPANIC ETHICS

Throughout this chapter, we have explored concepts from the Hispanic social location that inform how Latina/os reason about moral matters. Without question, for Latino/a ethicists to think about moral matters without these concepts is to separate themselves from their community. Unless ethical analysis is rooted in the Latina/o community, it is not Hispanic-based. Being ethnically Hispanic or having a Latina/o-sounding last name is not enough to do Latino/a ethical analysis. In an age when being Hispanic has become chic, especially for those under the false assumption that self-identification as a Latina/o scholar will somehow lead to more funding or teaching opportunities, there is a danger that the adoption of Eurocentric ethical paradigms will lead to the silencing, if not betrayal, of the voices of the Hispanic dispossessed and disenfranchised. No doubt some Latina/o ethicists may choose and feel more comfortable participating in Eurocentric ethical analysis. And of course, this is fine, and they should be encouraged to do so; but to switch to Hispanic-ness for the sake of convenience, or worse, profit, is both disingenuous and unethical.

As crucial as the community-based concepts—*lo cotidiano, nepantla, la lucha, en conjunto,* and *acompañamiento*—are for informing Latina/o moral reasoning, they are neither universal nor absolute. Notions of universality are usually constructed to privilege the subjectivity of Euroamericans (which they term objective) over and against the subjectivity of more marginalized populations. The ethical models arising from the Hispanic community are crucial for Latino/as. But we must take care not to romanticize Hispanic religious thought. Like all human endeavors, it falls short of the glory of God. On the other hand, although it is not "truth," it is unapologetically based on truth claims. Those seeking truth can find comfortable homes in the academy, but those seeking justice must begin their moral thinking in the insecure company of the marginalized.

Naturally, these disenfranchised communities never remain constant; they are always in flux. We must recognize, therefore, that as the Hispanic context changes, so must the methodology by which the community determines how to struggle for its dignity. Latino/a religious thought must constantly change to reflect the changing community from which it arises.

As crucial as concepts like *lo cotidiano, nepantla, la lucha, en conjunto,* and *acompañamiento* are to the Latina/o community, these concepts are several decades old. While it is true that the lack of academic excellence among many Euroamerican ethicists who have never heard of these terms, let alone understand them, is prevalent, Latino/a ethicists have been engaged in the same conversation occurring within the Hispanic community of yesteryear. The social location that produced these concepts has changed, and so must the Hispanic approach to these concepts. The concepts are not to be dismissed, for surely they remain relevant and useful in informing Latino/a moral reasoning. But I call on *la comunidad* to expand and further develop these concepts and to move beyond the way we are accustomed to think about moral matters, as well as to introduce newer ethical paradigms based on a radical activism focused on the liberation of Hispanics from the prevailing dominant social structures. To this task the rest of this book is devoted. Founding moral reasoning on these concepts, I will attempt in the next and final chapter to create a new ethical paradigm indigenous to the Hispanic social location.

4   WHERE WE ARE GOING

During the late 1950s on the streets of Chicago, in a Puerto Rican *barrio* called Lincoln Park, a street gang was formed, calling itself the Young Lords. Originally it was a turf gang that protected Hispanics (primarily Puerto Ricans) from other ethnic gangs. But the Division Street Riots of June 1966, a response to the shooting of a Puerto Rican by the Chicago police, changed the purpose and direction of the Young Lords.[1]

The shooting sparked an explosive situation mired in a history of police brutality against Hispanics. In addition, frustrations were high over the systematic evictions of Latina/o families because of gentrification, including the families of gang members. Among those incarcerated who participated in the riots was gang member José "Cha Cha" Jiménez. While in prison, he and other gang members read books by revolutionary thinkers and leaders, which contributed to their conscientization. The gang evolved into a political social movement with a Maoist-Marxist orientation that fought for and demanded basic human rights and better social services. By 1969, the Young Lords street gang was restructured as the Young Lords Organization, with groups meeting in Chicago and New York, as well as other major cities with substantial Hispanic populations. They focused on issues of gentrification, poor health services, and police brutality.

The New York chapter of the Young Lords launched the East Harlem Garbage Offensive on July 27, 1969. The Offensive consisted of sweeping the streets and neatly stacking up the garbage on the corners for pick-up. But the sanitation department historically ignored the accumulation of waste in communities of color and provided poor waste collection services. In response, the Young Lords moved the garbage bags to Third Avenue, a main thoroughfare used by commuters leaving Manhattan for the suburbs. There they built a five-foot-tall barricade across the avenue and set the garbage bags ablaze. Fighting broke out with the police when they attempted to stop the burning of garbage and arrest those responsible. This led to over 1,000 people marching to the 126th Street police station protesting the norm of police brutality. The Hispanic community was electrified as *abuelos* and *abuelas* lined the streets cheering. In spite of the crackdown by the police, the negative publicity caused by the protests prompted the city to be faithful to its responsibilities of picking up the garbage in Spanish Harlem, although the service never matched that offered in wealthier and whiter neighborhoods. Members of the organization also conducted a door-to-door campaign for lead poisoning and tuberculosis detection. Soon, the organization focused its energies on other institutions that failed to respond to the needs of the people they were supposed to serve, specifically the church, which has moral responsibility for protecting poor and disenfranchised communities. In 1969, Young Lords physically occupied the facilities of McCormick Seminary in Chicago (May) and *La Primera Iglesia Metodista Hispana* in New York City (December).

As Presbyterian ministers convened in Texas for a national conference in April 1969, the Young Lords (along with the Black Panthers, the Young Patriots,[2] and the Students for a Democratic Society [SDS]), aided by some McCormick Seminary students, staged a sit-in at the school's administration building. Barricading the doors, the protesters occupied the Chicago seminary for a week. The Young Lords voiced their grievances, specifically that Puerto Ricans were being displaced from the Lincoln Park community because of gentrification that was occurring with the complicity of the seminary. They demanded funding, to the tune of $600,000, for low income housing in the seminary's neighborhood, a children's center, a legal assistance program for residents, and a cultural center for Latin Americans. The protesters left the seminary when it agreed to their demands.

In New York City, *La Primera Iglesia Metodista Hispana* (First Hispanic Methodist Church), located at Lexington Street and 111th Avenue in the Spanish Harlem *barrio*, was visited by a delegation of the Young Lords requesting to use available space in the church to provide children in the neighborhood with a breakfast program and residents with a clothing drive. Even though the church was empty most of the week, the pastor, who was an anti-Communist Cuban exile, and the church board refused, referring to the Young Lords delegates as *satanás*—demons. When the Young Lords delegates attempted to address the congregation on Sunday, December 7, 1969, the church called the police, who showed up in the sanctuary and proceeded to beat the Young Lords brutally. On December 28, over a hundred Young Lords activists and sympathizers successfully took possession of the church, sealing the door with six-inch railroad spikes and raising a wooden sign with red letters renaming it *La iglesia de la gente*—The People's Church, under the premise that the first responsibility of the church is to the people. During the eleven days of occupation, over three thousand people came to church. The People's Church briefly developed childcare for working parents, established breakfast programs for children, conducted clothing drives, provided opportunities for political education, fought police brutality, and made a concerted investment in the social services (like health clinics). By January 7, 1970, the police had taken control of the church, arresting 105 occupiers—at which time the church ceased being the people's church.

Later that year, the Young Lords moved to take over Lincoln Hospital in South Bronx, the only health institution serving the needs of the predominantly Latino/a and African American community. Not surprisingly, the hospital had a history of ignoring their health concerns. So for twelve hours during the evening, the Young Lords occupied the hospital, demanding that the hospital provide door-to-door preventive health services, maternal and child care, drug addiction care, senior citizens' services, and increased minimum wage for hospital employees. The media attention given to the occupation of the hospital publicly revealed the substandard state of health care being provided to marginalized communities of color.

Unfortunately, because of F.B.I. infiltration of the organization and political infighting, the Young Lords disintegrated in the early 1970s. But for a brief moment, an indigenous Hispanic-based ethical methodology was enfleshed. The Young Lords were concerned that institutions, specifically religious ones, that played vital roles in the lives of Hispanics were abdicating the Christian mission they were professing to believe. Through their militant takeover and implementation of needed services, they demonstrated that those who claimed to perform the task of ensuring the people's welfare had violated their social contract. In effect, by implementing the services that should have been taking place, they shamed these institutions for failing to live up to their supposed mission. This was not civil disobedience, but rather civil initiative—forcing governments and institutions to live up to their rhetoric, a concept to be explored in greater detail later in this chapter. Although the Young Lords were not a Christian organization, nor were they practicing a pacifist ideology, they did demonstrate, more than most Christian theologians or ethicists, that the implementation of the gospel is a subversive and radical venture that disrupts, undermines, and challenges those who have become complicit with the status quo of oppressive structures. By their *jodiendo* in the streets, they modeled what a Latino/a ethical paradigm should look like. In the previous chapter we discussed the present state of Hispanic ethical thought. In this final chapter, we will attempt to move beyond current moral thinking by advocating an ethical paradigm of *jodiendo*.

DEFINING *JODIENDO*

I suggest that those of us who are Hispanic participate in a liberative ethics that I will call an ethics *para joder*. *Joder* is a Spanish verb, a word one would never use in polite company. Although it is not the literal translation of a certain four letter word beginning with the letter *f*, it is still considered somewhat vulgar and basically means "to screw with." The word connotes an individual who purposely is a pain in the rear end, who is purposely causing trouble, who constantly disrupts the established norm, who refuses to stay in his or her place. Why would I advocate an ethics that "screws" with the prevailing power structures? Because the disenfranchised, who must stand before the vastness of neoliberalism with little hope for radical change in their lifetimes, have few ethical alternatives. Regardless of the good intentions of those who are privileged by society, or the praxis they employ to paternalistically save Hispanics, the devastating consequences of empire will worsen as the few get wealthier and the many sink deeper into the despair of stomach-wrenching poverty. The dominant culture, including progressive ethicists, may be willing to offer charity and to stand in solidarity, but few are willing or able to take a role in dismantling the very global structures designed to privilege them at the expense of others. Hispanics occupy the space of Holy Saturday, the day after Friday's crucifixion, and the not yet Easter Sunday of resurrection. This is a space where some faint anticipation of Sunday's good news is easily drowned out by the reality and consequences of Friday's violence and brutality. It is a space where hopelessness becomes the companion of used and abused Latina/os. The virtue and/or audacity of hope become a class privilege experienced by those protected from the realities of Friday or the opium used by the poor to numb that same reality until Sunday rolls around. Regardless of the optimism they may profess, the disenfranchised, their children, and their children's children will more than likely continue to live in an ever-expanding poverty caused to benefit the empire's center. Sunday seems so far away. The situation remains hopeless, regardless of the skin pigmentation or gender of whoever the president of the empire happens to be.

No doubt, the Euroamerican reader of this text might also feel a certain twinge of hopelessness. After reading most of it, white readers may correctly sense, maybe for the first time, the irremediable gulf between them and Hispanics, and feel helpless and pessimistic. Can anything be done to address the concerns raised in this book that could possibly be sufficient to satisfy the Latina/o community? Quick and easy fixes may temporarily soothe one's conscience, but they are no substitute for bringing about a more just social structure, one not based on the disenfranchisement of Hispanics. Maybe at this time, all that can be asked is that our Euroamerican sisters and brothers sit by our side in the dust, as did Eliphaz, Bildad, and Zophar with Job, and accompany us in our hopelessness. But this hopelessness that I advocate is not disabling; rather, it is a methodology that propels toward praxis. All too often the advocacy of hope gets in the way of listening to and learning from the oppressed. Our Euroamerican sisters and brothers must sit with us for awhile in the reality of Saturday. The semblance of hope becomes an obstacle when it serves as a mechanism that maintains rather than challenges the prevailing social structures. Having no hope of vanquishing the empire's neoliberalism is never an excuse to do nothing. It may be Saturday, but that's no justification to wait passively for Sunday. The disenfranchised have no options but to continue their struggle for justice regardless of the odds against them. They continue *la lucha*, if not for themselves, then for their progeny. But how? By *jodiendo*!

When the disenfranchised start to *joder*, they create instability. Saul Alinsky probably said it best:

> *The first step in community organization is community disorganization.* . . . Present arrangements must be disorganized if they are to be displaced by new patterns that provide the opportunities and means for citizen participation. *All change means disorganization of the old and organization of the new.* (1971: 116; emphasis in original)

An ethics that upsets the prevailing social order designed to maintain empire is an ethics that can arise only from the margins of society, from those who are disillusioned and frustrated with normative Eurocentric values and virtues. While Euroamerican ethicists insist on social order, marginalized communities must call for social disorder, a process achieved by *jodiendo*. Perhaps it will lead some within the dominant culture to share in the hopelessness of overcoming the global forces of neoliberalism. If so, it will be the only way that progress is made. A liberative ethics *para joder* can be frightening to those who are accustomed to their power and privilege, because hopelessness signals a lack of control. And because those who benefit from the present social structures insist on control, sharing the plight of being vulnerable to forces beyond control will demonstrate how hope falls short. And perhaps this is the sad paradox: that hope can only be found after it is crucified and then maybe resurrected. For this is the hopelessness that was described in Paul's admonition to imitate Father Abraham, who "beyond all hope believed in hope" (Romans 4:18).

Any Latino/a ethics *para joder* is rooted in the foundational principles upon which Hispanics engage in moral agency—foundational principles elucidated in the previous chapter. Building upon this foundation, an ethics *para joder* moves toward a more subversive and radical response to oppressive structures than previously advocated by Hispanic religious scholarship. An ethics *para joder* refuses to play by the rules established by those who made the rules—rules that provide a space for orderly dissent that pacifies the need to vent for the marginalized but is designed not to change the power relationships within the existing social structures. If the goal of praxis is to bring about change, then it is crucial to go beyond the rules created by the dominant culture, to move beyond what is expected, to push beyond their normalized and legitimized experiences. Two examples can illustrate the implementation of this ethical paradigm. The first example is based on the praxis of an organization called

Católicos por la Raza[3] (Catholics for the People); the second has come to be known as the "Riverside Manifesto."

In 1969 Ricardo Cruz, a law student at Loyola Marymount University, began with others a political organization called *Católicos por la Raza* (CPLR).[4] CPLR protested how Catholic dioceses, specifically in Los Angeles, disproportionately spent their church funds on wealthier, whiter neighborhoods to the detriment of poor Latino/a neighborhoods. Additionally, the Catholic Church continued to ignore concerns raised by Hispanic parishes and refused to appoint Latino clergy to leadership positions. CPLR originally was organized to deal with the closure of Our Lady Queen of Girls High School, a predominantly Mexican American girls school; however, its first public protest occurred during the 1969 televised Christmas Eve mass at Saint Basil, located in Wilshire, where then cardinal James McIntyre spent almost $4 million on the celebration. Demanding that the Catholic Church be Christian, CPLR led a protest march, picketing outside the church during the mass. Several of the protestors made their way into the church, causing a melee that led to the arrest of twenty-one of them, including the organization's leader, Ricardo Cruz. According to Cruz, "Do we have to stay out of our own Church? A Church that is not only hypocritically wealthy, but which does not respect our culture. It is our duty, as Chicanos and Catholics, to return the Catholic Church to us" (García, 2008: 131). Cardinal McIntyre condemned the disturbance, which turned violent, from the pulpit, referring to the protestors as imitating the conduct of the rabble who at the foot of the cross shouted, "Crucify him!" Although the Christmas Eve disturbance led by CPLR was officially criticized as the "new barbarism" by the Catholic Church, the protest did contribute to the church's eventual appointment of several Hispanic cardinals throughout the southwestern U.S., to its making the Spanish language and Latina/o culture (specifically Mexican) part of the liturgy in Hispanic parishes, to a church-supported campaign for human development, and to the church's move to provide official support to organizations like the United Farm Workers.

The second example of an ethics *para joder* occurred some twelve years later, on March 12–14, 1981, when a major gathering on the urban ministry dubbed a "National Conference on the City" was held at the historic Riverside Church in New York City.[5] The conference was timed to celebrate the fiftieth anniversary of Riverside Church. Conspicuously absent from the scheduled speakers

were any Latino/as, who, ironically, because of economic disenfranchisement, were and are disproportionately engaged in urban
ministry. It is estimated that most of the 20 million Latina/os living in the United States in 1981 resided in urban areas, including
Spanish Harlem, several blocks from Riverside Church. On March
13, during one of the panel discussions held in the church's sanctuary, titled "Liberation Theology," a group of pastors, led by Benjamin Alicea, disrupted the proceedings by chanting "*¡Basta ya. No
nos pueden ignorar!* (Enough. You cannot continue to ignore us!).
Once the microphones were seized, the group proceeded to read
a document titled, "Complaints and Demands Presented to Main-
line Protestants, Conservative Fundamentalists and Establishment
Evangelicals at the Riverside Church Conference on the City." These
complaints and demands, which came to be known as the "Riverside Manifesto," were that (1) Latino/a communal social issues were
systematically ignored, not seriously addressed; (2) contributions
by Hispanics were ignored; (3) the religious establishment within
the U.S. needed to assume its share of responsibility for oppression;
(4) Latina/o liturgy and theology were denied their rightful place
within the U.S. religious community; and (5) Hispanics in theological seminaries and graduate schools of religion were discriminated
against. For many engaged in Hispanic religious scholarship today,
the "Riverside Manifesto" is one of those early praxes that disrupted
the status quo, establishing a space for our voices in future academic
conferences.

Obviously, the phrase an ethics *para joder* did not exist when
these events unfolded. I am aware that I am imposing a phrase of
my own coinage on historic events. Nevertheless, I will argue that
these events were led by individuals who refused to follow the rules
that usually ensure their people's subjugation to the dominant culture. We have evolved into a society that requires obtaining from
the police department a permit to picket the police department for
the brutality of the police department. We have freedom to protest,
as long as we do not disrupt the social equilibrium demanded by
those privileged with power, a social equilibrium morally justified
by those Euroamerican ethicists who benefit from those same structures of power. The only way for the powerless, the marginalized,
the disenfranchised, the dispossessed to counter the prevailing status quo radically is *joder*.[6] This becomes an ethics from the underside, an ethics that (1) is disruptive of social order and equilibrium;

(2) employs the cultural symbol of the Hispanic trickster in the formation of praxis; (3) gives honor to our holy *joderones* (screwers); (4) moves beyond civil disobedience toward civil initiative; and (5) is pastoral, constantly keeping the needs of marginalized communities at the forefront of any praxis employed.

A DISRUPTIVE ETHICS

Commenting on the writings of St. Augustine, Latin American ethicist José Míguez Bonino notes,

> [I]njustices should be corrected whenever that can be done *without endangering order and peace*. But if redress of wrong threatens to become disruptive, it should be avoided. The premise of Augustine's position in these cases is quite clear—peace understood as order. Society is an organization that must function harmoniously. The chief purpose of societal organization is the suppression of conflict and tumult. Changes, or the respect for personal freedom or for justice, might endanger that order. Whenever an alternative emerges, therefore, the Christian ought to work for the best possible solution, the most just and generous one, *short of endangering the existing order.* (1983: 83; emphasis added)

For Augustine, justice may be a major goal of the gospel message, but it must remain subordinate to social order. Bonino goes on to claim, correctly, that "Christian ethics—however idealistic—has operated 'at the service of the established order'" (84), a claim that was the thesis of the first section of this book. If it is true that Christian ethics as practiced is the ethics of empire, whose supreme goal is to maintain social order, then those claiming faithfulness to the biblical call for justice may need to bring about social disorder.

Ironically, when those in power have their power threatened, they call their disrupting of the status quo patriotic. When they kill, arrest, detain in internment camps, kidnap, torture, disappear, assassinate, or spread propaganda or engage in military conflict against whoever is labeled an enemy of democracy and "our way of life," they herald these actions as "our fight for freedom," which of course is never free. Those in power always understand the means by which they maintain their power as ethically rooted in the highest virtues and values. Thus they make terms like *justice, patriotism, equality,* and *law and order* meaningless. But when the disenfranchised employ similar means to wrestle power away from the dominant culture, they are labeled as angry, hostile, unethical, immoral, and un-Christian. Radical activist Saul Alinsky probably said it best: "There can be no such thing as a successful traitor, for if one succeeds, he becomes a founding father" (1971: 34).

Who would not cherish communal harmony? Unfortunately for Latino/as relegated to the *barrios* of this nation,[7] police brutality,[8] violence,[9] underemployment and unemployment,[10] dilapidated schools,[11] poverty,[12] inadequate housing,[13] incarceration,[14] and a lack of adequate health care[15] prevent harmony from taking root within our communities. As the above examples concerning the Young Lords illustrate, attempts to change radically the status quo are met with difficulties, if not hostility. For empire to function at full efficiency, an undereducated, underemployable reserve army of laborers is needed both in the Global South and in the midst of the empire itself. Not surprisingly, this reserve army is disproportionately of color, as national unemployment statistics verify. The economic structures of neoliberalism, embedded in racism and ethnic discrimination, are beyond reform. What is required is a radical economic change, specifically in how the earth's resources are distributed.[16] Of course, those who benefit from the present arrangement may willingly participate in charity, but they remain unwilling to move toward any type of justice that questions or threatens their power, possessions, or privilege. It is always easier to write a fifty-dollar check to feed the hungry; it is a different matter and far more difficult to ask how our protected privilege within empire causes hunger throughout the world.

Complicating the situation is the practical inability of the dispossessed to bring about the downfall of empire or neoliberalism. Those whom the dominant culture privileges have all the necessary resources (including political power and military technology) to protect by any means necessary their privileged space. Maybe in some distant future, the internal contradiction of capitalism will accomplish this task, but for the here and now, the options are limited and dismal. Because of the futility of directly challenging the dominant culture, and the historical fact that those in power have never willingly abdicated it, I would argue that the course of action available for the marginalized is proactively to disrupt existing oppressive structures through an ethics *para joder*.

The Young Lords Organization disrupted the status quo, the social equilibrium advocated by ethicists of the dominant culture.

For their praxis of justice they were beaten and arrested. To a great extent, they were dangerous because the disruption unmasked the hypocrisy of those in power who were supposed to serve and protect the disenfranchised. Yet an ethics *para joder* does not sponsor *jodiendo* for its own sake. It is an ethics that calls for *jodiendo* with the express purpose of disrupting the stranglehold on the marginalized. Immanuel Kant may have given those in power the categorical imperative[17] on which to base their moral reasoning, but for those for whom the categorical imperative does not apply, there is the relational imperative, the basing of moral action upon a reflection that can only occur when one is in relationship with the oppressed and marginalized. The Young Lords and other Hispanics seeking a more relevant ethical paradigm move away from Kantian abstractions by rooting moral agency in lived relationships among the disenfranchised. The call to burn the uncollected trash of the Hispanic neighborhoods on Third Avenue, a street used by those escaping to the "safety" of suburbia, was a disruptive ethical act of *jodiendo* that came to be because those carrying out the act were in relationship with those harmed by the city's refusal to collect the trash regularly. The issue is not whether trash burning on the city's major intersections should become a universal law. Those in white neighborhoods who have grown accustomed to regular trash pickup may wish to frame the issue this way, but it is ludicrous to propose that those forced to live in their filth seek to remedy the problem with such methods. For the Hispanic marginalized, the decision to participate in disruptive ethical acts of *jodiendo* is communal, based on the consequences that not acting, not disrupting the precious equilibrium of the dominant culture, would have on relationships within our Latina/o *comunidad*.

To advocate disruption of the status quo is to assume that those engaged in this form of ethical activism are fully aware of how power works, functions, and operates—how power reveals while it conceals. An ethics *para joder* is based on a critical analysis of power. It recognizes that power is not centralized in the hands of a few elites; instead, power exists everywhere, pulsing through institutions, traditions, customs, and everyday practices defined as normal. As French philosopher Michel Foucault reminds us, "Just as the network of power relations ends by forming a dense web that passes through apparatuses and institutions, without being exactly localized in them, so too the swarm of points of resistance traverses social stratifications and individual unities" (1978: 96). The most mundane, unassuming act is pregnant with power relationships. Every institution or human interaction, formal or informal, is a locus from which power and resistance flow, benefiting some and not others. It is a power that cannot be possessed, only exercised. Because power cannot be limited to the realm of the elite, replacing the elite with members from disenfranchised communities would not suffice to eliminate these networks ingrained in every fiber of American life. The autonomy of power is structured and designed to punish any dissenter from the norm, even those among the elite. Those who exercise power are not necessarily aware of their complicity with the overall power relationships and their self-subjugation to those relationships. If those within the dominant culture make a preferential option for the disenfranchised Hispanic, the very structures that are designed to privilege them will then work to marginalize them.

Any Hispanic-centric ethical analysis must be fully aware that the power of empire is most potent in its ability to traverse and produce ethical paradigms, for power constructs knowledge and produces discourse. Power produces reality and creates its subjects' opinion of what is "truth" (Foucault, 1984: 60–61). This is a power that is tolerated if it is able to mask a substantial part of itself (Foucault, 1978: 86). At times this power is well masked, undetected by those engaged in the everyday. Unfortunately, when it comes to dealings between agents of the dominant culture and Hispanics, this hidden and at times not-so-hidden display of power can be quite coercive. But for the coerciveness associated with the exercise of power to be most effective, it must appear natural and neutral. Thus, it appears natural and neutral for the Catholic Church to spend millions on a Christmas Eve service while closing down a Hispanic girls' school for lack of funds, or for Riverside Church to hold a conference on urban ministries a few blocks from the Latino/a urban *barrio* without ever thinking of including their voice.

Within the field of ethics, power relationships are often masked by how the dominant culture defines its ethical paradigms. It creates a series of opposing systems to define what is good, moral, and acceptable and what is evil, immoral, and unacceptable, and thereby distinguishes between what it determines should be legal and what it determines should be illegal, what is criminal and what is noncriminal. The dominant Eurocentric culture's power to construct definitions of moral agency can undermine the quest of marginalized communities—in our case, Hispanics—for liberation from oppressive power relationships. If the crossing of an artificially constructed border created through the U.S. conquest of Mexican land is illegal, then any discourse concerning immigration policy is trapped within a construct in which those who cross borders are by definition "illegal" aliens. Those with the power to define set the discourse, to the detriment of those lacking that power, who should be the subjects, but instead are reduced to mere objects. Achieving justice becomes more difficult because the dominant culture has used its power to name and frame any ethical discussion on this issue.

For the disenfranchised to participate in an ethics *para joder* will mean that their methodology will be in conflict with an ethic complicit with empire and the power of empire to define the moral standards by which all are required to live. Combating what has been legitimized and normalized forces the moral agent to move beyond how the dominant culture has come to define the good. When the Hispanic marginalized engage in a disruptive ethics that subverts and challenges normative Eurocentric definitions of the moral, their actions will be viewed with horror and disgust by those engaged in an ethical analysis that maintains the equilibrium of the empire. Physically taking over churches, seminaries, and hospitals will be viewed negatively by those wishing to preserve a social order that protects their privileged space. Consequently, to disrupt the norm, *joder*, becomes a moral imperative.

Yet some would argue that an "extreme" militant praxis, such as taking over institutions to unmask oppressive structures, is crossing a societal line, making the praxis unjustifiable. After all, doesn't the Hispanic community live in a freer society than previously, a democracy in which they can participate in the political arena to bring about change? Didn't the election of President Obama bring about a postracial America where the barriers that maintain repressive structures have been torn down? For Hispanics to live within the borders of the United States is to consent to the principle of their own subjugation while hoping that the empire, manifested as the American dream of upward mobility, will radically provide salvation from their present estranged existence. Hence, by accepting the dream, the dreamer furthers his or her own disenfranchisement. Although Latina/os are told they are "free" to pursue their destiny, in reality they remain subjugated within the illusion of freedom by what appear to be benign social structures. During the July 2009 Senate confirmation hearings on the nomination of Judge Sonia

Sotomayor to the U.S. Supreme Court, Democrats consistently heralded her as an example of the American dream fulfilled, of a person who, in spite of growing up in a disenfranchised Latino/a community, could, just like anyone else, simply lift herself up by her bootstraps. In reality, she is the exception to the rule—not the norm. The vast majority of Latino/as in this country with an economic background similar to Sotomayor's will, more than likely, live a life of menial labor, economic hardships, and few opportunities. Nevertheless, by raising Sotomayor upon a pedestal to serve as the paragon for all Hispanics living under economically oppressive conditions, the dominant culture maintains the illusion of the American dream that anyone "can make it if she works hard enough." And of course, when the vast majority are unable to grasp the success offered by that illusion, proponents of the American dream myth lay the blame on the Hispanic for not working hard enough. They never consider whether disenfranchisement of Hispanics might be necessary for the enrichment of the dominant culture.

We can understand this dynamic through the concept of *panopticon*. Panopticon describes a prison designed by eighteenth-century social theorist Jeremy Bentham. The prison was conceived in such a way that it allowed the prison guard to observe the prisoners without the prisoners being able to detect whether they were being observed. According to Bentham, panopticon would be "a new mode of obtaining power of mind over mind, in a quantity hitherto without example" (1787 [1843]: 39). The prison's center would contain a guard tower from which the guard could gaze at the prisoners in their individual backlit cells. The prisoners would be unable to return the guard's gaze because the tower would be darkened. The guard's gaze would confer power to him or her as observer while becoming a trap to those observed, even when the surveillance was not constant. The mere possibility of being watched would force the prisoners, as objects, to internalize the power relation. In effect, they would learn to police themselves. Foucault builds on Bentham's prison when he writes,

> He who is subjected to a field of visibility, and who knows it, assumes responsibility for the constraints of power; he makes them play spontaneously upon himself; he inscribes in himself the power relation in which he simultaneously plays both roles; he becomes the principle of his own subjection. By this very fact,

the external power may throw off its physical weight; it tends to
the non-corporal; and, the more it approaches this limit, the more
constant, profound and permanent are its effects: it is perpetual
victory that avoids any physical confrontation and which is always
decided in advance. (1995: 202–3)

Panopticon is a mechanism that exercises power, and it can serve
as a model of how oppressive power works in keeping Hispanics
self-policed while living in a free society. At one time there may
have been laws and customs that overtly segregated people of color,
including Latino/as. I am old enough to remember "for rent" signs
in Miami Beach that would say, "No Children, No Cubans." My
hermano/as on the West Coast faced similar signs: "No Dogs, No
Mexicans." Our ethnic identity determined the schools to which
we were relegated and the neighborhoods in which we could live.
But laws since then have been changed for the better, and political
correctness has come to reign supreme. And yet, the experience of
the majority of Latina/os is still segregation—in the schools they
attend,[18] in the neighborhoods where they live,[19] in the type of jobs
they hold.[20] Why? If indeed we live in a free society in which laws
no longer segregate us, why do we remain segregated? Because, I
will argue, the vast majority of people of color, including Hispanics, freely self-imprison themselves within the artificial walls of
panopticon.

When a police officer brutally attacks a Latino, when a Hispanic
is dismissed from employment unjustly, when the refusal to provide
adequate services to neighborhoods predominantly occupied by Hispanics is normalized, when thousands die in the desert attempting
to cross artificially constructed borders, when a Latina must provide
sexual favors to obtain legal immigration status or a job to feed her
children, then the abuse that overtly targets one "offending" Hispanic is symbolically directed at all potential Latino/as who might
dare to step out of line and request *dignidad* and *justicia*. For this
reason, the display of abuse or punishment must be seen or known
by all within the targeted community, while masked and hidden
within the dominant culture. Its being masked in the dominant culture provides that culture with an excuse to feign ignorance and
thus dismiss accusations of abuse as hyperboles voiced by "angry"
Latino/as leftist, or to say that if such abuses did occur, they were
perpetrated by rogue individuals. Still, physical and institutional

violence reminds Hispanics of the triumph and legitimization of the Eurocentric norm.

In a perverse way, the violence faced by Latina/os becomes a religious ritual designed to purify the whole society from all of its ills: unemployment, crime, drug abuse, crumbling economy, and poor health services, to name but a few. "If it wasn't for those damn spics. . . ." You can fill in the rest: ". . . taking our jobs"; ". . . using up our social services"; ". . . refusing to speak the language"; ". . . importing crime"; ". . . bringing diseases"; etc., etc., etc. Violence provides for the sacrificial death of the Hispanic, who carries the sins of those who defile what has been defined by Euroamericans as good. The sacrifice of the Hispanic provides life, and life abundant, for those whom society privileges.

The abuse and disenfranchisement faced by Hispanics bring into play the lack of symmetry between the Latina/o who dares to go against the good as defined by the Eurocentric culture, and the constructed all-powerful will of the dominant culture, which displays its strength to communicate what will happen to those who refuse to conform to the "ethical truth" as established and defined by Euroamericans. By maintaining the status quo, that culture does not intend to establish justice, but rather to manifest power, and, through that power, to preserve the prevailing power relationships. Maintaining the existing social structures by any means necessary at times requires a not-so-well-masked demonstration of physical violence. This violence, visited upon the few, is always directed toward all Hispanics. Hence, it is not a mechanism that prohibits, that says "thou shall not"; it is a mechanism that produces, that produces political and social subservience. For self-policing to be effective, Latina/os must know about the possibility of physical and/or institutional violence, because all must be made afraid; and all must bear witness to its infliction so as, to a certain extent, to partake in its unleashing. The efficiency of the prevailing U.S. power relationships can be measured by the minimum use of brute force it requires and by its ability to rely instead on Hispanics, cognizant of the consequences of nonconformity, to accept and recognize the prevailing norm and the cost and futility of defying that norm.

With time, segregation laws are no longer needed to maintain segregation. Like the punishing guard of panopticon, these weapons have been effectively used in the past, and the guard's ubiquitous gaze has been internalized. A shift in the "technology of power" takes effect when yesterday's tortured and abused public bodies of Latina/os become today's docile private bodies confined to their individual "cells." As the eyes of Hispanics committed to memory the terror caused by nonconformity, a system of diminishing penalties took effect. Instead of brute force, public ridicule or ostracism became sufficient to ensure Latina/o obedience. Even though the dominant culture may still occasionally find it necessary to use brute force as a reminder, in general it has shifted its exercise of power, from the exclusionary laws and techniques employed in the past toward a reliance on self-policing within the sociopolitical hierarchy.

An ethics *para joder*, even though it arises from marginalized Hispanic spaces, is also an ethics from which power flows. Ethics is the power to perform praxis that creates reality. If one of the goals of an ethics *para joder* is to disrupt the status quo, to disrupt the equilibrium in society that those in power need in order to remain secure in their privileged positions, then probably the best figure to bring about this disruption is the trickster. Tricksters are known for creating situations that lead to new ways of dealing with the discord produced by their tricks. Society masks oppressive structures by legitimizing and normalizing the status quo. This makes resistance to the present social order appear futile, as both those who benefit and those afflicted are lulled into complicity. The trickster, as the ultimate *joderon*, disrupts the norm to force those being tested to seek new options, opportunities previously unrecognized. In addition, the trickster raises consciousness, possibly leading oppressors to repent and move toward a more liberative way of living that can result in their own salvation. Because the trickster plays an important role in providing opportunities for liberative praxis, it is to the trickster we now turn, the trickster as basis for the construction of an ethics *para joder*.

A TRICKSTER-BASED ETHICS

Ethical analysis normatively operates along a good-evil binary structure. Either you are with the forces of good (i.e., God), or you are aligned with the forces of evil (i.e., the devil). Based on a Eurocentric deductive formula for shaping praxis, the privileged Euroamerican's quest for "the good" becomes foundational in determining what moral actions she or he should take. Unfortunately, history testifies that in fighting evil, people sometimes cause more evil, and occasionally their actions in defense of the good lead to greater atrocities than those they had opposed. We have seen in the first section of this book how pursuing the good has justified empire and its oppressive death-causing results. A world where the good is defined through the reasoning and/or experience of those with power to legitimize and normalize how they define the good is a world where the marginalized can hold little hope for justice, because ethical perspectives derived from the center of empire usually cause more evil than good for marginalized communities. Any moral framework that causes harm, if not death, through institutional violence to the Latina/o community must be declared immoral, for it stands in direct opposition to the mission of Christ, which is to give life and give life abundantly (John 10:10).

A prevalent theme within Western moral thought is an either/or rationalism that clearly demarcates good from bad. How then can one incorporate the both/and ambiguity common in the messiness of life? If this good-evil dualism proves ineffective in analyzing moral agency, then what paradigm is available for Latino/as? How can we best capture the ambiguity of a Latina/o moral agency that recognizes the need at times to dispense with personal piety for the sake of the greater good of survival—survival of not just the individual Hispanic, but more importantly, *la comunidad*? One Hispanic cultural symbol on which a methodology for ethical analysis can be based, but that until now has been overlooked by some within the Latino/a community, is the ambiguous figure of the trickster. The mythical character of the trickster is amalgamated with the social reality of Latina/os to unmask external oppressive social structures under which Hispanics are forced to live and the internalization of those same structures into the Latino/a psyche. An ethics *para joder* relies on the trickster figure to challenge external oppression and uncover its internalized manifestation. Tricksters allow us to suspend strict Eurocentric paradigms and definitions of morality, what is right and what is wrong, to provide us the opportunity to study and comprehend how social structures are constructed to the detriment of our people. Furthermore, tricksters are rule breakers, and thus employ a praxis that is needed if the marginalized are to break free from the rules that hold them in a subordinated space.

James C. Scott, in his book *Domination and the Arts of Resistance*, proposes that the trickster operates within a public sphere of a group politics of disguise and anonymity intended to convey double meanings even as it provides a space for the powerless to speak with authority to power while shielding their identity. The trickster's tales may appear harmless or comical, but for those whose social location is marked by disenfranchisement and oppression, these become stories that celebrate the cunning wiles of those who navigate an environment set on their destruction. Yet in spite of the treacherous traps set against the trickster, in the end, the trickster triumphs over the more powerful (1990: 162–66). How? By studying the weaknesses and negative habits of the more powerful and by employing humor, deceptive methods, lies, or passive aggression.

Hispanics living within the empire, faced with traditions and regulations that foster their destruction (e.g., immigration laws, English-only ordinances, unfair hiring practices, etc.) have few options but to develop tactics and strategies to help them cope and survive. I will argue that in the creation of an indigenous Latino/a ethical paradigm, the trickster figure can provide Latina/os with a survival paragon to emulate. Although trickster figures in the Latino/a imagination are woven from *lo cotidiano* of Hispanics, they are still difficult to define or describe. Generally speaking, tricksters are characterized by ambiguity, transformative power, and razor-sharp wit. They are marginalized figures that are usually unpredictable and inconsistent, occupying the space of both hero and villain.

In Victor Turner's study of trickster figures, he characterized them as "liminal" (from the Latin *limen*, "threshold"). Tricksters stand at the threshold of cultures, breaking down old categories to bring about new possibilities (1969: 125–28). The trickster, like Latina/os, has one foot in one world and the other foot in another. Both Hispanics and tricksters are threshold (border) crossers, forced to break down the reality in which they find themselves so that they can survive, cognizant that in deconstructing, they make new liberative opportunities and possibilities available. In most Hispanic traditions this breakdown of existing power relationships is done with humor; hence, not surprisingly, their tricksters are usually portrayed as jokers or pranksters. Their uncanny ability to survive against insurmountable odds is masked by a clownish or childlike demeanor. The trickster relishes disrupting the norm, causing chaos so as to outwit those who view themselves as superior, and in so doing, revealing their hypocrisy. Trickster tales usually portray the trickster as physically weaker than those out to destroy him or her; yet the trickster refuses to be relegated to the margins of society and destined to play a passive role within social structures. Being less powerful than the oppressors bent on domination, the trickster is forced to rely on deception to exploit the oppressor's false sense of self-righteousness, which usually masks greed for power, privilege, possessions, or any combination thereof.

Trickster figures radically subvert established norms that attempt to preserve the traditional moral values and virtues that undergird empire. They stand over and against the power relationships established by the dominant culture. The trickster figure could therefore prove to be an important ethical symbol for liberative moral agency. As an agent of chaos, yet a source of culture, the trickster transforms individuals and society. Because Hispanics realize that direct challenges to existing social structures (although necessary at times, as illustrated by the Young Lords Organization) will usually lead to violence against them, if not their demise, they employ forms of deceptive and cunning resistance, whereby their chances for success could be improved. Before we consider how the trickster figure could function in the conduct of Latina/o ethical analysis, we must first determine whether the trickster figure is a common cultural symbol within the Hispanic *comunidad*.[21] I argue, yes. Fortunately, several figures known among Latina/os can be understood as tricksters.[22]

Usually the trickster figure occupies a sacred space. Among Afro-Caribbean religious traditions there are stories about the quasigod (*orisha*) named Eshu, whose origins can be traced to Yoruba (present-day Nigeria). Eshu is also known as Elegguá among followers of Santería, Exu in Brazilian Candomble, Legba in Caribbean vodou, and Lucero in Palo Mayombe. Of all the *orishas*, Eshu is the most cunning. Two of his stories illustrate how he operates to overcome those who are more powerful and brings down the haughty.

Eshu's older brother, Oggún, god of war and iron, would visit his parents' house regularly, especially when his father, Obatalá, was not home. He would usually kick Eshu out of the house, lock the doors and shutter the windows, and then proceed to rape their mother Yemmú. Unable to bear the shame, and realizing his inability to overcome physically the mightier Oggún, Eshu conceived of a plan to trick his father and put an end to Oggún's abuse. After being thrown out of the house again, Eshu ran to the yam fields where Obatalá was tilling the soil. "Come quick, *baba-mí* [daddy], I thought I heard *iyá-mí* [mommy] crying and fear she might have hurt herself." Obatalá hurried back home, and when he burst into the house, he discovered Oggún in the midst of his reprehensible act.

Fearing his father's wrath, Oggún begged to curse himself, which he did, swearing to work for all eternity without rest until he paid the debt of his ignominy. Also, he agreed to reveal the secret of iron to humanity, thus ceasing to be god over the metals. Obatalá also punished his wife, removing her youngest child, Changó, from her presence and swearing to bury alive the next child from her womb. Finally, Obatalá rewarded Eshu by making him the god who would always be the first to be fed among the gods. Through deception, Eshu was able to confound a more aggressive foe and earn a reward in the process.

Another Eshu story reveals how tricksters humble the haughty. Obi, the god associated with the coconut used for divination, was a favorite of the Creator, Olofi. Obi was renowned for his sincerity, so Olofi made him pure white and set him high atop the palm tree. Unfortunately, Obi's newfound honor made him conceited. To prove the point, Eshu threw a party at Obi's house, but only invited the poor. When Obi came home and saw his home filled with the disenfranchised, he threw them all out in disgust. Eshu then approached Olofi and told him that something might be wrong with Obi. Maybe if he showed up at Obi's house disguised as a beggar, Olofi would discover how Obi's elevation in status was affecting him. Olofi followed Eshu's advice. When Obi saw the beggar, he treated him rudely until Olofi revealed himself, cursing Obi from that day forward to fall from the palm tree and roll around in the dirt. His beauty would be hidden; thus the obi (coconut) is brown on the outside and white on the inside. Furthermore, he would be used by rich and poor for divination purposes. Again through deceit, Eshu puts the arrogant in their place.

Tricksters are also portrayed as small cunning animals able to outwit or fool a more powerful persecutor. A popular tale from the Andes focuses on the adventures of Quwi (or Cuy) the guinea pig,[23] who constantly outfoxes Tío Antonio the fox. For example, one day while rummaging for food near a large boulder, he sees Tío Antonio approaching. With no place to hide and unable to outrun the fox, he quickly finds a part of the boulder that juts outward. Quickly he presses his arms up against the bottom of the overhang. As the fox prepares to pounce and devour Quwi, the guinea pig asks if the fox has heard the news: the sky is falling, and he is holding it up with this large boulder. The fox gets concerned. What if it's true? Then Quwi asks for a favor. He hasn't used the bathroom all day;

would the fox mind holding up the sky for a few minutes while he goes to relieve himself? The fox agrees, and Quwi gets away.

In some cases the trickster is a jokester, usually portrayed as a mischievous child. Humor is liberatively used to provide the marginalized hearers with much needed laughter to deal with their own struggle for survival. Also, jesters are able to question through humor what is defined as normative, creating a space for possible change. The jokester temporarily frees himself or herself and the hearer from existing social restraints due to overarching power relations. Proper decorum is suspended, and the social morals, values, and virtues of those who benefit from maintaining proper decorum are rejected and/or subverted.

Probably the best known trickster stories among different Hispanic ethnic communities (e.g., Dominicans, Guatemalans, Puerto Ricans, Cubans, etc.) are the stories of Pepito (Little Johnny). Pepito is sometimes portrayed as a small, humble simpleton who usually confounds the more powerful through childish innocence. Many Latino/a ethnic groups have Pepito stories; others have a similar figure but with a different name. It would appear that these stories were brought to Latin American countries by the Spanish colonizers. A childish jokester such as Pepito operates within a realm of formal assumptions about who is superior and who is inferior, assumptions enforced through proper etiquette and behavior. Although consigned to inferior status, the jokester Pepito is able through either his innocent demeanor or his razor-sharp wit to switch the roles and thereby unmask the shortcomings of those who perceive themselves as better or of a higher social status.

To illustrate how the jokester subverts assumptions concerning who is superior and who is not, we can briefly review some of the common tales. Among Cubans, for example, there is a tale of Fidel Castro elaborately describing to a group of school children the differences between the communism of La Habana, where they lived, and the capitalism of Miami, where the *gusanos* (maggots) emigrated. He described La Habana as a paradise where everyone shared the goods of society and lived happy and content. This he contrasted with Miami, which he described as corrupted by the greed of politicians leading the majority of the people into poverty and misery. After finishing his diatribe, Fidel noticed that Pepito was gently sobbing. "What is wrong, Pepito?" asked the *Comandante*. Pepito responded, "I want to live in La Habana!" Thus in this story, Pepito's childish innocence says to power what the people, out of fear, are not able to say, and in so doing, calls power to take its own rhetoric seriously.

As can be imagined, some of the Pepito stories are a bit racy. For example, Pepito walks into the crowded doctor's office and tells the receptionist that there is something wrong with his penis (of course, a more vulgar word is usually used when recounting this story). Shocked, the receptionist states that such words should not be used in polite company lest he embarrass the ladies or gentlemen who might be present. She tells Pepito that he should have said something was wrong with another part of his body, like his eye or ear, and then discussed the real problem in the privacy of the doctor's office. She then sends Pepito outside and asks him to try again. Pepito leaves, only to return saying that there is something wrong with his ear. Feeling satisfied that Pepito has been put in his place, the receptionist smugly thanks him for the information and asks him what is wrong with his ear. Pepito responds that he can't urinate out of it. In this story, the hypocrisy of those who consider themselves better is humorously unmasked.

Among Puerto Ricans there are stories of another little boy similar to Pepito. He is called Juan Bobo (John Dummy). Like Pepito, Juan Bobo is able to make social commentaries through his childish innocence. Among the most popular stories about Juan Bobo is one that concerns his mother's instructions to take their pig to market and sell it. To ensure a high price, she asks Juan Bobo to clean up the pig and make it look beautiful. Having cleaned the pig, Juan Bobo feels it is not yet beautiful. Going to his mother's closet, he finds her prettiest dress and places it on the pig. Using his mother's cosmetics, he puts eye shadow, mascara, and lipstick on the pig. Determining that the pig now looks beautiful, he takes it to market, but on the way the pig spots a muddy puddle. As could be expected, the pig throws itself into the middle of the puddle and begins to roll around, destroying the clothes it is wearing and smearing the makeup. Eventually Juan Bobo pulls it out of the mud and takes it to market, but when he arrives, everyone laughs at the sight. And thus was born the popular saying about people who in trying to put on airs get so dressed up they become unrecognizable. They are said to be "all dressed up like Juan Bobo's pig."

Among Mexicans there is Don Cacahuate (Mr. Peanuts), also a simpleton, who through humorous social entanglements manages to survive. For example, one day his wife asks him to make her a *bolillo* (a bread roll), to which Don Cacahuate responds, "How can I make you a *gringo* if I'm Mexican?" *Bolillo* has a double meaning. It literally means bread roll, but it is also a disparaging term used for Euroamericans. Hence, without realizing it, Don Cacahuate speaks against assimilation, for it is not possible for a Mexican to make, or become, a Euroamerican.

A precursor to Don Cacahuate is Pedro de Urdemalas or Pedro Ordimales, literally Peter Mischief-Maker. Stories concerning Pedro date to the late twelfth century, although the character was made popular in the comedic writings of Miguel de Cervantes in the early seventeenth century. Well known throughout the Spanish-speaking southwestern U.S., he is a bit more *picaro* (streetsmart) than Don Cacahuate. A critic of the status quo, he is constantly out-witting his supposed superiors for his own gain. According to one of the tales, Pedro, while walking a dirt road, is saddened by the sight of wealthy men in fine clothes upon beautiful stallions constantly passing by. So Pedro takes a large block of wood and carves a don-key. He waits until a fine gentleman approaches to begin mounting the wooden animal. The gentleman stops him and inquires what he is doing. Pedro explains that this is a magical donkey that becomes flesh and is faster than any other beast in the world once mounted. Wanting the best and fastest, the gentleman offers to buy the beast, but Pedro refuses. After much haggling, Pedro agrees to exchange the donkey for the gentleman's horse, his fine clothes, and the gold in his pocket. As Pedro begins to ride away he tells the gentleman that the magic only works when no one is around. So the gentleman, pen-niless and dressed in rags, waits until Pedro rides off before mounting a wooden donkey that does nothing. Hence Pedro tricks the rich by using their greed for conspicuous consumption against them.

Probably the best known modern day Hispanic trickster is the internationally known Mexican film star of the 1940s and 1950s, Cantinflas.[24] A social satirist, he made popular the *pelado* (plucked one), a clownish character of the 1920s who appeared in theater groups. Cantinflas as *el pelado* is the comical vagabond and underdog who insultingly says the truth that everyone else is thinking about his or her supposed superior. He became famous for a style of speak-ing known as "Cantinfleada." Whenever he was in trouble with the authorities, was trying to woo a beautiful woman, owed someone money, or was in danger of physical violence, Cantinflas would begin a normal conversation that would then become so obfuscated that no one understood what he was saying. Thus he could insult and humiliate the person with whom he was speaking, without that person knowing what was happening. This form of trickery entered the Spanish dictionary (*Real Academia Española*) in 1992 as the terms *cantinflear, cantinflas,* and *cantinflada.* The *pelado* character that Cantinflas perfected became a major figure in skits performed by *El Teatro Campesino* (the Farmworkers' Theater),[25] where through humor consciousness was raised concerning serious political and social issues.

Finally, there are tales with pseudo-Christian heroes as tricksters. For example, in "The Pongo's Dream," a Quechua version from Peru (believed to have Indic origins), an indigenous servant works on the *hacienda* of a cruel *patrón.* One day the meek servant shares a supposed dream he had about the *patrón.* According to the dream, the two of them died. The *patrón* was dipped in honey, while the indigenous servant was dipped in manure. St. Francis appeared in the dream condemning each to lick the other for all eternity.

Among the most popular Hispanic religious figures is *la virgen de Guadalupe.* Although not necessarily considered a trickster in the traditional sense, she still disrupts and turns the traditional church hierarchy on its head. She supposedly appeared to a poor indigenous peasant, Juan Diego, in 1531, approximately one decade after the Spanish conquest of Mexico. Rather than appearing in the colonial capital to the highest ranking religious figure, this the manifestation of the divine appeared to an insignificant poor and oppressed Indian on the hill of Tepeyac, not speaking Christian (Spanish) but the tongue of those considered to be pagans. Salvation, rather than coming from the official colonized church to the presumed infidels, came from these so-called nonbelievers to the church.

These few examples of Latina/o tricksters illustrate the genre as symbolizing social protest, thus resonating with the marginalized hearer and providing psychological release of built-up tension, resentment, and anger through laughter. One of the traits common to all of these Hispanic-based tricksters is their disregard for prevailing rules and regulations. Why do they conduct themselves this way? Because they realize that the prescribed social order exists to maintain and legitimize the privileges of the few at the expense of many. Tricksters lie so that the truth can be told. When they lie, cheat, joke, and deceive, they reveal a deeper truth obscured by the moralists of the dominant culture. Although the means used by the trickster to achieve liberative ends may not be considered moral by the dominant culture, the trickster is ethical, operating in a realm that moves beyond good and evil—what society defines as being right or wrong. In short, the trickster is a *joderon* (a screwer) who at times may appear noble, but in all honesty, can also be vengeful or ruthless.

The trickster as consummate survivor can serve as an exemplar for disenfranchised Hispanics, who also need to find ways of surviving the reality constructed for them. By disrupting the empire's equilibrium to create compromising situations for those in power, the trickster is able to reveal their weaknesses, expose what they prefer to keep hidden, and remove their artificial masks of superiority. The trickster's trials and tests force the powerful to consider the spiritual consequences of their actions. Disrupting the norm creates new situations that can provide the marginalized with fresh ways of approaching their oppression. By opening new paths for the disenfranchised, the trickster can provide opportunities to seek different solutions not previously considered and investigate possible alternatives previously unexplored. The trickster's significance lies in prompting new ways of thinking that can be liberating and insightful.

How then can the trickster figure be reconciled with an inherited Christian faith, whose Eurocentric manifestation has minimized or eliminated any references to such a figure? I would argue that those on the underside of Eurocentric Christianity, who are struggling to survive, will identify with stories of tricksters, not only those tales from popular culture explored above, but also tricksters who appear in the Bible. A reading of the Bible reveals a prevalent literary genre of the trickster, somewhat ignored by those of the dominant culture, but identifiable by the disenfranchised.

We find biblical tricksters in the form of the patriarchs of the faith. Abraham tricked both the Egyptian Pharaoh and King Abimelech of Gerar into believing that his wife was his sister, thereby acquiring financial gain (Genesis 12:10-20; 20:1-18); his son Isaac attempts to pull off the same trick with King Abimelech of Gerar (Genesis 26:1-11); and then there is the weaker Jacob, who tricks his older and more powerful brother Esau out of their father's blessing (Genesis 27:1-45). But even the trickster can get tricked, as in the case of Laban, Jacob's father-in-law, who tricks Jacob out of seven years of labor and the woman he wants to marry by switching brides on the wedding night (Genesis 29:15-30). During Egyptian captivity, the Hebrew midwives Shiphrah and Puah lie and deceive the

Pharaoh to save the lives of the Hebrew babies (Exodus 1:15-21). The Hebrews are then tricked by an elaborate scheme perpetrated by the Gibeonites to enter into a treaty of nonaggression (Joshua 9:3-20). In the book of Judges there is Ehud, who tricks Eglon the King of Moab into a secluded room so that he can kill him and free his people from tyranny (Judges 3:12-30); Jael also frees her people by providing Sisera deadly hospitality (Judges 4:17-22); and there is Samson, who through his riddles tries to achieve personal gain, only to be tricked himself by his wife Delilah in the end (Judges 14; 16). Then you have King David, who feigns madness before King Achish of Gath to preserve his life (1 Samuel 21:11-14). And there is his son King Solomon, who tricks two women fighting over a baby into being truthful by suggesting he will cut the baby in half (1 Kings 3:16-28). These tricksters, these *joderones*, these screwers with the established order, engaged in deception to achieve personal gain (Jacob), survival (David), salvation of their people (Shiphrah, Puah, Jael, and Ehud), and truth (Solomon).

The tricksters of the Bible provide those who face overwhelming odds against survival with a moral justification for the employment of deception as a means of self-preservation. Although a thorough examination of the biblical text to uncover the many manifestations of trickster figures and their importance to the development of the Judeo-Christian faith is a worthy project, it is beyond the scope of this book. It will suffice to say that the trickster figure is prevalent in the Bible. Still, two biblical figures that might require closer attention for our purposes are Jesus and Satan.

Because Jesus Christ is a liberator, he is a *joderon*, one who screws with the established political and religious authorities by subverting the legitimacy they have constructed. And for this, he pays the ultimate price of crucifixion, accused of being a heretic. Jesus *el joderon* screws with those who have established themselves as the political and religious leaders of the people and who from their lofty positions screw the very people they are entrusted to represent, support, and protect. By employing an ethics *para joder*, Jesus screws up their plans for oppressing the people. Cleansing the temple becomes a liberative praxis that literally overturns the established tables. To be imitators of Christ is to do likewise, *joder*.

The other biblical trickster figure worth mentioning is Satan. While Jesus represents the paragon of the *joderon*, Satan represents a more ambiguous manifestation of *joderon*. Satan's trickery can lead us to deeper truths about ourselves and our mission. Take the example of his attempt to tempt Jesus in the wilderness. Having fasted for forty days and forty nights, Jesus was weak and hungry. Three times Satan tried to test (trick) Jesus. The first test was with possessions: "Command that these stones may become bread" (Matthew 4:3); then with privilege: "If you are the Son of God, throw yourself down" (Matthew 4:6); and finally with power: "I will give all these [kingdoms] to you if you fall down and worship me" (Matthew 4:9). As trickster, Satan tests Jesus with the temptations faced by most humans, unearned possessions, privilege, and power, but Jesus rises above the tricks; and in so doing, thanks to Satan, Jesus learns something about himself and his mission. Only after the testing can Jesus begin his ministry with a clearer understanding of his goals. To believe the deception of tricksters like Satan, rather than rise above it, can lead to ruin. The consequences of our response to tricksters never depend on the trickster, but rather on us.[26]

Looking at the trickster quality in both Jesus and Satan demonstrates that the role the trickster plays can lead to good, usually manifested as conscientization, among the oppressed and possibly their oppressors. But tricksters can also lead people toward their own destruction. *Joderones* create situations in which the one being tested can rise to the occasion, recognizing that Christ, who is with her or him, has already overcome the world. Or the one being tested can fall short of the challenge by clinging to his or her more base instincts, which can lead to greater misery as grace is refused.

How then can this trickery concept be manifested within the church? One way can be illustrated by something that occurred during the mid-1990s when I was conducting field research at a Hispanic Pentecostal church in Paterson, New Jersey. In this particular church, women were not allowed to preach or stand behind the pulpit. The church held a very conservative view about women's place in the home, the church, and society. But even though they were supposed to remain silent, they found their voice when filled by the Spirit. While attending a baptism service of adult believers, I witnessed the Spirit as a trickster. When the men were baptized through immersion, they emerged from the waters shouting *gloria a dios*, or some other short praise phrase. But when the women were baptized, the Spirit came down upon them. Filled with the Spirit, these women began to preach, something prohibited under normal circumstances. But it was not they who were preaching, but the Spirit through them. And what message did the Spirit have for the congregation? The Spirit, through these women, publicly made known the women's grievances against the men in the church. One woman preached against some men who were beating their wives. Another woman held a man cheating on his wife accountable for his sin. And still another spoke of the need for men truly to love their wives as Christ loves the church. The baptism service, followed by the presence of the Spirit speaking through these women, lasted for almost an hour. The trickster (whether the Spirit or the women themselves) was able to subvert the male dominance of the congregation that required women to remain silent. The women were able to lash out at their oppressors without experiencing retaliation or taking responsibility for the words they spoke because it was not them making the accusations, but the Spirit of the living God speaking through them. Under the cloak of being filled with the Spirit, grievances and demands that normally would have no place to be heard can be made in a public forum during the performance of a sacrament.

HOLY *JODERONES*

The term *saints* refers to humans who have been beatified and canonized by the Catholic Church because the church deemed them worthy of honor and devotion for the virtuous life they lived or the martyrdom they willingly accepted. But while the official church has its saints, the people venerate their own. These saints are individuals who emerge from struggling communities and whose intercession is sought by the people, even though the official church does not recognize them, individuals like César Chávez or José Martí.

Some of these saints could be individuals who may not have necessarily lived virtuous lives. In fact, they may have participated in actions contrary to Eurocentric sensitivities concerning the ethical. Nevertheless, the ambiguity of their lives can incorporate a trickster-type persona. Take for example the people's saint Jesús Juárez Maso, also known as Jesús Malverde. He has been revered throughout northern Mexico for nearly a century and has become a popular icon in the United States since the start of the twenty-first century, particularly in California and the southwest. According to folklore, Jesús Malverde was a Robin Hood–type bandit who stole from the rich and gave to the poor. He was killed in 1909 by the police. With time, people began to believe that his image offered protection from the law. Many migrants venerate the image of Jesús Malverde, praying that he will provide either safe passage into the United States or money once they arrive. While traversing the migrant trails through the mountains, I came across several crevasses along giant boulders converted to altars where the image of Jesús Malverde, along with the images of other folk saints, was placed. His main shrine is located in Culiacan, Sinaloa, believed to be his birthplace. It is visited frequently, and many who visit it attribute miraculous healings to his intercession. Many drug dealers have begun to pray to him for protection, making him their patron saint, or, as he is sometimes called, the "narco-saint." Still, there are those who repudiate his association with drug dealers, insisting that the people's saint is being misappropriated.

If we dismiss the misappropriation of the saint by drug dealers, we are left with a bandit who stole from the rich to provide for the needs of the poor. Traditional ethics, categorizing thievery as a vice, could never consider Jesús Malverde a role model for the people, worthy of either emulation or veneration. Nevertheless, because of oppression, the most ethical response to situations in which one has few alternatives is purposely to break the current law. For the undocumented who are forced out of their homeland because of the U.S.' foreign trade policies and need for cheap labor, as well as because of their own country's mismanagement of resources, alternatives are limited. To obey the law and stay where they are can lead to institutional violence and hunger, if not death. Or they can break the law and seek a new opportunity to satisfy basic needs for their family. If they choose the latter, they need the protection and guidance of a saint who understands breaking laws. Malverde is an appropriate saint because, like the people who venerate him, he exists in that ambiguous space between right and wrong, where such categories betray the position of power and the advantage those who hold it have, which allows them to determine and define right and wrong. What the people need to survive are bandit saints, who seek the greater good of defending the right to provide the hungry with food, rather than the morality of the elites, who are more concerned with protecting property rights, specifically for their property.

ETHICS OF CIVIL INITIATIVE

Liberative ethics argues that theological and theoretical reflections are derived from praxis, turning on its head the Eurocentric deductive ethical paradigm, which first begins with theory as "truth" and then moves to praxis as the implementation of that truth. As liberative ethicists point out, the truth believed by the dominant culture is a construct reflecting the bias and prejudices of that culture, which, consciously or unconsciously, developed ethical paradigms that are complicit with empire and fall short of calling for radical changes in how wealth, power, and privilege are disbursed. For ethics to be authentic, for ethics to be closest to the biblical mandate, it must arise from disenfranchised communities that are reflecting on the praxis they are employing in order to survive. To that end, an ethics *para joder* incorporates civil initiative—a concept developed by the hermeneutical circle for ethics, specifically as it is presently being integrated along the U.S.' southern border as a methodology that brings to light the human rights violations taking place against the undocumented. Ethics as civil initiative as opposed to civil disobedience is an ethical concept that arose years earlier as a reflection on praxis being implemented during the 1980s Sanctuary Movement. This was based upon the praxis employed by houses of worship to protect Central American refugees from deportation to the death squads, torture chambers, and civil wars of El Salvador and Guatemala.[27]

How is civil initiative different from civil disobedience? Martin Luther King Jr. operated during a period when laws prohibited African Americans from full citizenship and participation in society. King initiated civil disobedience as a strategy by which unjust laws are purposely and publicly violated by those willing to assume the consequences of their disobedience in order to raise society's consciousness in the hope that it will be moved to change unjust laws. The civil disobedience initiated by King proved successful in motivating the passage of legislation designed to provide equal access and protection. Inequalities remain, but the problem is no longer bad laws, but rather how the good laws that were enacted are followed or ignored.

During the Sanctuary Movement of the 1980s a move away from King's civil disobedience had to be made. Those fighting for the rights of Latin Americans entering the U.S. to escape death in their countries of origin did not want to change U.S. refugee laws, because they conformed to international standards. The problem was not with the laws, but with the U.S. government, which was violating its own refugee laws by refusing to recognize those fleeing persecution in Latin America. It was the government who was committing a perverted form of civil disobedience. The goal was not to do away with bad laws, but to force the government to follow good laws that existed. A new term and strategy were required. Jim Corbett, a Quaker activist and one of the cofounders of the Sanctuary Movement, reflecting upon the praxis the movement was making, developed the term "civil initiative" to put into words the praxis that participants in the movement were carrying out. "Civil Initiative is the legal right and the moral responsibility of society to protect the victims of human rights violations when government is the violator" (Fife, 2009: 172).

Civil initiative is based on international law, specifically the legal response developed during the Nuremberg trials of Nazi officials who tried to exonerate themselves from blame for a multitude of atrocities with the excuse that they were "simply following orders." The court, in *United States v. Goering* (1946), concluded that international duties transcend individual obligations to obey national states. There is a moral obligation to help victims of human rights violations. Today, probably the greatest human rights violation within the U.S. borders is occurring against Latino/as on those borders. Not since the days of Jim and Jane Crow has the U.S. government maintained a policy that systemically brings death to a group of people based on their race or ethnicity. Our immigration policies are killing Hispanics. As our people constantly remind us, this is not a border that separates the U.S. from Latin America; it is a bleeding scar caused by the Third World rubbing up against the empire.

This "scar" was predicted by a 1993 report titled "North American Free Trade Agreement: Assessment of Major Issues," prepared for the U.S. House of Representatives by the U.S. General Accounting Office. Even before the trade agreement's ratification, the report predicted a rise in immigration over the next decade (1994–2004) in response to the implementation of NAFTA. When Euroamericans say that our present immigration policy is broken, they refuse to acknowledge that it was purposely broken to benefit the empire. Dumping the U.S. surplus of subsidized corn (at about $4 billion per year from 1995 to 2004) on Mexico meant a 70 percent drop in Mexican corn prices and a 247 percent increase in the cost of housing, food, and other essentials. Not surprisingly, over one million Mexican farmers lost their land within a year of NAFTA's ratification. Our trade policy pushes migrants out of Mexico, while our hunger for cheap labor, labor that native-born Americans do not want to do, pulls them toward the U.S. But rather than acknowledge our complicity in causing undocumented immigration, and rather than work toward a comprehensive and compassionate immigration reform, we responded to the predicted increase in immigration by implementing Operation Gatekeeper the same year we ratified NAFTA (De La Torre, "Introduction," 2009a: 37–44).

Until then, most migrants crossed into the U.S. through urban centers like San Diego, Nogales, and El Paso. Operation Gatekeeper sealed the border at these traditional entry points, pushing the trails through inhospitable mountain ranges and deserts. Operation Gatekeeper was based on the assumption that migrants would die crossing the desert. Thousands did die. These "collateral damages," it was believed, would deter other migrants thinking of making the dangerous crossing. What we know is that no one was deterred. The Mexican economic shambles, to which we contributed, forced desperate people to face any obstacle in the hopes of being able to send money back home to feed their hungry children ("Introduction," 2009a).

Civil initiative becomes a Hispanic-centric ethical response developed by those doing feet-on-the-ground ethics. Some of us convicted by faith, others moved by humanitarian inclinations, have gone to the desert to leave food and water on the migrant trails. We are doing what international law states the U.S. government should be doing. Furthermore, we are recognizing that international duties transcend our individual obligation to obey our national states. Not to sound trite, but as one of the posters of the organization No More Deaths succinctly states that humanitarian aid is not a crime. When we play a cat and mouse game with the Border Patrol in order to place water and food on the trails, as well as provide medical aid, we are *jodiendo*, we are "screwing" with the officials. When we were detained by the Border Patrol for a short time, our camp being raided in the late morning, we offered them lunch, simply *para joder*.

A PASTORAL ETHICS

It is important to end this book by stressing the underlying motivation for *jodiendo*. One does not *joder* for the sake of *jodiendo*. That is, one does not disrupt or subvert purely for the sake of disrupting or subverting. Such an approach could lead to unsettling consequences that could deepen the disenfranchisement of Latina/os. While calling for revolutionary changes, we must remain leery of revolutions, for all too often, Saturn becomes its god and Robespierre its prophet.

Any praxis employed must be *en conjunto* with the disenfranchised community and for the sake of the marginalized, specifically for the sake of raising consciousness, and for the sake of challenging and slowing down the empire. If praxis creates greater burdens for the marginalized instead of a more liberative alternative, then maybe the strategy will need reassessment. An ethics *para joder* never comes from above, but from below. Because this is an ethics from below, from the margins, it has a crucial pastoral dimension. Those who employ an ethics *para joder* are activists with pastoral concerns, that is, putting the liberation of the disenfranchised first.

Because Latino/a liberative ethics *para joder* comes from below, it seldom fits in the proper, refined settings of historic seminaries or pristine churches. It is a vulgar, earthy way of doing ethics—a method that requires getting dirty. What makes it vulgar is not the usage of the word *joder*, but the vulgarity of how the vast majority of Latina/os are forced to live in this country. I attempted to fashion an ethical response that would resonate with the majority of real people of flesh and blood, not high-minded intellectuals. Hence, I propose an earthy ethics because it arises from the Hispanic community, because it is not created in ivory towers that conjure abstract definitions of the good or of virtue. To accompany marginalized Latina/os in their struggle for survival requires getting one's hands dirty. To be a scholar-activist means standing against empire. At times, this may require loss—loss of livelihood, loss of freedom, maybe even loss of life, for to share in the lives of the marginalized means sharing in their fate. Loss is not sought, but at times it may become the consequence of *jodiendo*. Euroamericans enjoy the privilege of driving to a march. To get arrested for some movement earns them a badge of honor. But for disenfranchised communities, arrest is a frequent risk of living as a person of color. There is no need to go out and seek direct confrontation with the authorities just for the sake of seeking confrontation, to prove how liberal we are. Confrontation is the possible consequence of engaging in liberative ethics, but we do not seek it. Why? Because confrontation takes the focus and resources away from the disenfranchised and places them with those seeking to prove their activism. Like tricksters, we avoid confrontation even though it is always a constant companion in the doing of justice.

It is fitting to end where we began, by asking the question, What happens when you fry baloney? Only by accompanying the marginalized can those seeking their salvation find the answer. We may now know that it bubbles up, but we still need to know why the disenfranchised have to know that answer. An ethics *para joder* becomes a proactive way of participating in bringing about a justice that might one day make the answer to this question irrelevant. Until that day, we continue to eat and share our fried baloney.

NOTES

PREFACE

1   The author has supplied all biblical translations from the Greek original.

2   The usage of the term *empire* to describe the United States' position within the world order will more than likely make conservatives and liberals bristle. Such a description of the U.S. is usually dismissed as hyperbolic rhetoric, the common parlance for the "blame America first" crowd. Yet, if we recognize that the concept of empire is no longer limited to physically possessing foreign lands forced to pay tribute to a militarily superior nation, then the term is appropriate. Empires of old were defined by how much land their armies could control; today, control is not measured by boots on the ground but by economics. The term has evolved to encompass the globalization of the economy by one superpower to provide multinational corporations with economic benefits, with capital gains secured and protected by a military might depicted as necessary for justice and peace. Like the Roman Empire of old, the United States Empire secures a *pax americana* so that the elite leaders of the empire, and their counterparts within dominated countries, can reap benefits, usually at the expense of the vast majority of the world's marginalized. Modern-day empires can arise only through the existence of foreign and domestic disenfranchised groups that provide both raw material and cheap labor. The wealth, prosperity, and power of the center were dependent on the exploitation of the groups of people that existed on their margins. Economic structures and relationships create and heavily influence societal power relationships. Those who resided in what is commonly called the "Third World," with its enormous human and natural wealth, provided the material resources necessary to transform the United States, whose economy was anemic at the start of the twentieth century, into the sole superpower at the close

of that century. Non-European land, resources, and labor, obtained through exploitation of those who lacked military and technological superiority, existed to enrich the center. Unfortunately, military or technological superiority has come to be confused with cultural, intellectual, and religious supremacy.

CHAPTER 1

1   According to Gary Dorrien (2003), the phrase "blacks of the South and the seething yellow flocks beyond the Pacific" appeared in an 1895 pamphlet titled *What Shall We Do with the Germans?*

2   It is interesting to note that when the Teutonic races fought each other during the First World War, Rauschenbusch was less militaristic in his views.

3   It is important to note Edward W. Said's elucidation of how the term *Orientals* has historically been used to portray Asian men as feminine and weak and as known for their sensuality, cruelty, and despotic nature. See his classic text *Orientalism* (1979).

4   Although Rauschenbusch accepts and supports the initial actions of American imperialism, by the time of the First World War he moves away from the jingoism he initially advocated, even to the point of calling for the Philippines' independence.

5   In his final book, *A Theology for the Social Gospel*, published during the First World War, Rauschenbusch, disheartened and demoralized by the war between his beloved Germany and the United States, calls for the social gospel to move beyond national injustices and inequality toward international issues like imperialism and nationalism. "All whose Christianity has not been ditched by the catastrophe [of the Great War] are demanding a christianizing of international relations. The demand for disarmament and permanent peace, for the rights of the small nations against the imperialistic and colonizing powers, for freedom of the seas and of trade routes. . . . Before the War the social gospel dealt with social classes; to-day it is being translated into international terms" (1917: 4).

6   Thistlethwaite argues that women are particularly tempted to submerge their individuality, their self, to the needs and desires of others—a temptation facilitated by the Niebuhrian private/public dichotomy.

7   One last personal note: in 1959 Niebuhr wonders if Cubans would have been "better served by our continued sovereignty over the island" (24–25). As a Cuban, I must respond that our dilemma is a direct result of the U.S. physically invading our country four times to set up governments friendly to U.S. business interests that controlled the vast majority of the Cuban economy and wealth; two covert operations to overthrow the Cuban government—not to mention the infamous Platt Amendment—have also contributed to our problem. He admonishes Latin America for its inability to establish stable

democracies; to do so is, he judges, "beyond [their] present capacity" (1959: 159). Yet he fails to acknowledge how many Latin American democracies were overthrown by the U.S. for economic gains. In reality, Cubans would not have been better served by the Marines invading one more time. Niebuhr's inability to recognize that his version of a benevolent empire is the cause of the Cuban predicament, not the savior of the Cuban people, makes his ethics irreconcilable with the Cubans' quest for justice.

8   It should be noted that what concerned Hauerwas about liberalism was its questioning of the truthfulness of the Christian narrative and its proclivity toward a civil religion.

9   Gloria Albrecht asks a similar question, pointing out how Hauerwas' church is rooted in, and continues to adhere to, patriarchy and authoritarianism, ignoring those whom it has disenfranchised. Hauerwas fails, according to Albrecht, to consider seriously how power operates within the church to the detriment of those marginalized by the church:

> Hauerwas [does not] question the power relations that actually exist within church communities and the effective silencing of voices that might challenge the views they assume. Essentially, the authority-of-clergy vs. the authority-of-community debate . . . conceals the reality that authority in either case lies within the hands of (predominately white) male clerical or (predominately white) male communal leadership. The obvious problematic consequence for women and men of color is that an authentic understanding of scripture requires submission to the authority and discipline of a (white) male dominated institutional church, its self-defined traditions, its seminaries, and its professional disciplines. Nonetheless, Hauerwas . . . argue[s] that only by this authority and under this discipline, Christians learn to "see" their world. Without this authority, we do not "see" as Christians. (1995: 49–50)

10   Hauerwas seems to think that Gutiérrez's approach to liberation is Kantian and, as such, "does not sufficiently guard against" the Enlightenment project, which seeks freedom "from all servitude" in the hopes of becoming "artisans of our own destiny" (1986: 69; 1991: 50–52).

11   It is interesting to note that John B. Thomson's book, *The Ecclesiology of Stanley Hauerwas: A Christian Theology of Liberation* (2003), attempts to argue that Hauerwas' theological work is in fact a distinctive kind of liberation theology. Thomson masterfully demonstrates what a liberation theology constructed from the social location of the privileged and powerful, as opposed to the disenfranchised and oppressed, would look like.

12   Justice is a bad idea for Christians, Hauerwas argues, because "a theory of justice" that provides the means to know in principle what

justice qua justice entails does not exist. To ground justice in some abstract right or contractual agreement distorts the moral capacity of Christians. Not having a definition for justice means that such discourse is really more a product of the Enlightenment project than of the witness of the Christian church (1991: 68).

13   "Act only on that maxim whereby thou canst at the same time will that it should become a universal law" (Kant, 1785 [2008]: 39). Hence, the categorical imperative leads us never to treat humanity merely as a means but always simultaneously as an end.

CHAPTER 2

1   Patrick Buchanan's speech was delivered at the 1992 Republican National Convention, Houston, TX, August 17, 1992.

2   "Today we march, tomorrow we vote."

3   In 1933 the administration of Franklin Roosevelt implemented the Good Neighbor Policy to replace the previous gunboat diplomacy of Theodore Roosevelt. Rather than "speaking softly and carrying a big stick," the U.S. attempted more subversive means by which to influence Latin America, including, but not limited to, (1) supporting strong dictators and providing them with military training, (2) covert operations when needed, and (3) control of financial structures, especially through unfair trade agreements and providing loans.

4   Stephen Dinan and Ralph Z. Hallow, "Conservatives Slam Split Race Rulings," *Washington Times*, June 25, 2003.

5   Timm Herdt, "Groups Ask: Who Gave the Money?" *Ventura County Star*, July 10, 2002.

6   See Focus on the Family, http://www.family.org/cforum/citizenmag/features/a0036727.cfm. This Web site is no longer active.

7   David Lerman, "District Lawsuit Argument to Begin, Black-Majority District Challenged," *Newport News*, September 11, 1996.

8   http://www.spiritualprogressives.org/.

9   I was approached by the leaders of the Colorado Democratic Party to make a presentation during one of their regional conferences on how to deal with the immigration issue from a religious perspective.

10   It is important to note that while David Gushee places Campolo and Wallis in the Religious Left, he situates Sider within the Religious Center camp (2008: 92).

11   Nicholas Dirks argues that British colonialism transformed India's caste system to facilitate control of the country. The caste system, as we know it today, is not a relic of ancient India, but a colonial form of civil society (1989: 59).

12   There is James Dennis, who would have preferred killing Sider rather than talk to him because he was white (1993: 22–23); there are Michael and Addie Banks, who fail to see the connection between their lack of salvation and their "racial prejudice" that leads to

"self-destructive bitterness and anger" (81–82); and there is angry Tim Brown, who spirals into poverty because of the slight of a racist supervisor (1999: 78).

13 Ronald J. Sider, "An Evangelical Theology of Liberation," *Christian Century*, March 19, 1980, 314–18.

14 Space prohibits me from thoroughly analyzing Sider's lack of a hermeneutical suspicion. For a more in-depth analysis on how marginalized communities approach and read Scripture, see my earlier work, *Reading the Bible from the Margins* (2002).

15 See Funding Universe, http://www.fundinguniverse.com/company -histories/GULF-amp;-WESTERN-INC-Company-History.html.

16 For a complete discussion of *han*, see Andrew Sung Park, *Racial Conflict and Healing* (1998).

17 Jim Wallis, "Biblical Politics," *PostAmerican*, April 1974, 3.

18 Jim Wallis and Robert Sabath, "The Spirit in the Church," *PostAmerican*, April 1974, 4.

19 Jim Wallis, "No Peace, No Honor," *PostAmerican*, April 1975, 4.

20 Jim Wallis, "The 'Outsider' in the White House," *Sojourners*, January 1978, 3.

21 Jim Wallis, "George W. Bush's Theology of Empire," *Sojourners*, September–October 2003, 20–26.

22 It should be noted that one of then senator Obama's speeches on the connection between religion and politics was printed in *Sojourners*, November 2006, 8–16.

23 Jim Wallis, "A New Faith Coalition," *Sojourners*, January 2009, 5.

24 Wallis, "New Faith," 5.

25 The other four spiritual advisors are Rev. Otis Moss Jr. (civil rights veteran), Rev. Joel C. Hunter (pastor of a conservative megachurch), Bishop T. D. Jakes, and Rev. Kirbyjon Caldwell (these last two both entrepreneurial ministers). See Laurie Goodstein, "Without a Pastor, Obama Turns to a Circle of 5," *The New York Times*, March 15, 2009.

26 Jim Wallis, "America's Original Sin: The Legacy of White Racism," *Sojourners*, November 1981, 15–17.

27 Jim Wallis, "America's Original Sin: The Legacy of White Racism," *Cross Currents*, Summer 2007, 197–202.

28 "Dom Helder Camara," *Sojourners*, July/August 1976, 17–19. Dom Helder Camara would be featured many more times throughout the years, even having an entire issue focused on him. The following month the magazine focused on Latin American liberationist thought and included the voice of Samuel Escobar, a Latin American evangelical liberationist.

29 "Fighting for Our Lives," *PostAmerican*, May 1975, 3–4.

30 In *Sojourners*, October 1977, see "Gaining Justice Ground," 18–20, and "An Interview with César Chávez," 21–25.

31   From 1971 to 1983, with over 130 issues, there have only been three articles dealing specifically with Hispanic issues (one of which was on the 1980 Sanctuary Movement, which is really a response to aggression by the U.S. against Latin American countries), one interview with a Latino (César Chávez), and one article written for the magazine by a Latino/a—Dolly Arroyo—dealing specifically with a Hispanic-centric issue. It should be noted that Arroyo, who described herself as having "latent Latin blood" ("For Lack of a Green Card," *Sojourners*, June 1982, 27), has occasionally contributed to the magazine since February 1981, but with one exception, she has mainly written on non-Hispanic topics. Not included in these numbers are short news briefs involving Hispanics, under the title "For the Record" (five counted); book reviews written by Hispanics (one counted by Orlando E. Costas); and books written by Latina/os that were reviewed (zero counted). I arrived at these numbers by physically examining every issue of *PostAmerican* and *Sojourners* published since their inception.

32   In that year, there were three articles dealing specifically with Hispanic issues (again, two of which were on the 1980 Sanctuary Movement) and one interview with a Latino or Latina (on undocumented refugees), but no articles by Latino/as dealing specifically with a Hispanic-centric issue.

33   Lorraine Granado, reviewed Ada María Isasi-Díaz and Yolanda Tarango's book *Hispanic Women: Prophetic Voice in the Church* (Harper & Row, 1988) in an article titled "Emerging Voices: Hispanic Women and Liberation Theology," *Sojourners*, December 1988, 34–36. The next time a Hispanic-centric book was reviewed was the next year. Reviews of Hispanic-centric books authored by Latina/os became more regular after 1992.

34   Consuelo Sague, a pediatrician, joins others in a discussion on abortion and the law in her essay, "Neither Murder nor Liberation," *Sojourners*, November 1989, 21. After that, Latino/as started to appear in other forums, the next being two years later in "1992 Rediscovering America," *Sojourners*, October 1991, 16.

35   Some articles begin to deal with Hispanic issues, like Florida farm workers (Aurora Camacho de Schmidt, "Field of Lost Dreams," *Sojourners*, June 1990, 34–35), LA gang members (Greg Boyle, "Deadly Despair: An Inside Look at Gang Activity in Los Angeles," *Sojourners*, October 1990, 30–31), and U.S. political prisoners (Naomi Thiers, "The U.S. Government Policy and Practice of Political Imprisonment Is Designed to Intimidate," *Sojourners*, May 1991, 16–23).

36   Lillie Rodulfo, "Speaking the Language of News: The Influence of the Hispanic Media in the United States," *Sojourners*, August–September 1992, 37–38.

CHAPTER 3

1   García earned his Ph.D. from the University of Chicago under the supervision of James M. Gustafson in 1982. The title of his dissertation was *The Concept of Justice in Latin American Theology of Liberation*. He has been a professor of Christian Ethics at Austin Presbyterian Theological Seminary since 1986, specializing in the intersection of Christian ethics and issues of social justice. In 2010 he retired.

2   Villafañe earned his Ph.D. from Boston University under the supervision of Paul K. Deats in 1989. The title of his dissertation was *Toward an Hispanic American Pentecostal Social Ethic, with Special Reference to North Eastern United States*. Since 1976 he has taught Social Ethics at Gordon-Conwell Theological Seminary, where he focuses on a contextualized urban theological education that addresses ministries in the inner city and incorporates the needs of urban pastors and Christian leaders.

3   Isasi-Díaz earned her Ph.D. from Union Theological Seminary under the supervision of Beverly Harrison in 1990. The title of her dissertation was *En La Lucha—In the Struggle*. She has taught at Drew University, Seminario Evangélico de Teología (Matanzas, Cuba), Dayton University, and Ewha Womans University (Seoul, South Korea). Her areas of specialization are Christian social ethics, mujerista/Latina/o theology, feminist theology, and feminist ethics. In 2009 she retired.

4   Mendiola earned his Ph.D. from the Graduate Theological Union under the supervision of Karen Lebacqz in 1991. The title of his dissertation was *Autonomy, Impartial Rationality, and Public Discourse: A Theological Proposal*. He taught Christian ethics at Pacific School of Religion, where his research focused on bioethics and sexual ethics, with particular reference to lesbian, gay, bisexual, and transgender people. Mendiola passed away in 2008.

5   I earned a Ph.D. from Temple University under the supervision of John Raines in 1999. The title of my dissertation was Ajiaco *Christianity: Toward an Exilic Cuban Ethic of Reconciliation*. I taught at Hope College, moving to the Iliff School of Theology in 2005. The focus of my scholarship has been social and political ethics within contemporary U.S. thought, specifically how religion affects race, class, and gender oppression. I specialize in applying a postmodern/postcolonial social theoretical approach to U.S. marginalized spaces to construct a theological and biblical ethics that challenges structures of oppression.

6   See *Mañana*, 1990.

7   See *Our Cry for Life*, 1993.

8   See *Galilean Journey*, 1983.

9   The first book ever written specifically on Hispanic religious thought

was Antonio M. Stevens Arroyo's book *Prophets Denied Honor: An Anthology on the Hispanic Church in the United States* (1980). By 1990, only six books dealing with the Hispanic religious experience were in print. During the 1990s, books focusing on Latina/o religious thought started to appear more regularly. By 2000, about fifty-five books (since the 1980s) that dealt with the Latina/o religious experience were published, all authored by this first generation of Hispanic religious scholars.

10   Among the few notable Hispanic-centric books written by Latino/as are the following: Ada María Isasi-Díaz, *En la Lucha* (1993); Eldin Villafañe, *The Liberating Spirit* (1993); Ismael García, *Dignidad* (1997). Although I, along with a generation of Hispanic ethicists, am grateful for the space these pioneers carved out for us in the academy, it will become abundantly clear in the next chapter that I am proposing a new and different direction—a direction that no doubt will create controversy both within and without the Latino/a *comunidad*.

11   Even my own award-winning book, *Doing Christian Ethics from the Margins* (2004), is not Hispanic-centric, but rather draws from many disenfranchised and dispossessed communities to create a more inclusive method for conducting ethical analysis. The Hispanic ethical perspective is just one of many explored by the text.

12   For a detailed understanding of the development of the concept of *lo cotidiano*, see Carmen M. Nanko-Fernández, "Cotidiano, lo" (2009a: 158–60).

13   For a detailed understanding of the development of the concept of *nepantla*, see Lara Medina, "Nepantla" (2009a: 403–7).

14   For a detailed understanding of the development of the concept of *la lucha*, see Ada María Isasi-Díaz, "la Lucha" (2009a: 335–37).

15   For a detailed understanding of the development of the concept of *en conjunto*, see Daniel R. Rodríguez-Díaz, "Teología en Conjunto" (2009a: 761–72).

16   In 2006 and 2007, "Hispanics were two and a half times as likely as Whites to receive a higher-priced loan" (27.6% of Hispanics, 10.5% of whites). The recent economic downturn resulted in substantial loss of wealth for Hispanics, as "more than three in five (62%) Latino homeowners saw foreclosures in their neighborhoods in 2008" (National Council of La Raza, 2009: 1–2). A major source of household and communal disruption is the disproportionate incarceration rates of Hispanics. Even though "Latinos represented almost 13% of the U.S. population in 2000, they constituted more than 31% of incarcerated individuals in the federal criminal justice system that year." Even more, "Hispanics have one chance in six of being confined in prison during their lifetimes" (Walker et al., 2004: vi). The psychological trauma inflicted on Hispanics is also telling: "According to a 2000 study by the National Council of La Raza and the National

Association of Hispanic Journalists, less than 1% (0.53%) of network television news stories focused on issues related to Hispanics. Of these stories, 80% focused on just four topics—immigration, affirmative action, crime, and drugs—stories in which Latinos were likely to be portrayed in negative roles" (4). Additionally, a 2003 report by the Bureau of Justice Statistics showed that over 41% of state and federal inmates had not completed high school or its equivalent. In fact, 53% of Hispanics in state prisons had not completed high school or its equivalent either, compared to just 27% of non-Hispanic whites (Harlow, 2003: 1).

17 For a detailed understanding of the development of the concept of *acompañado*, see Roberto S. Goizueta, "Acompañado" (2009a: 3–5).

18 For a detailed understanding of the development of the concept of Hispanic Christology, see Luis G. Pedraja, "Christology" (2009a: 589–98).

19 The Eurocentric Christ is not only detrimental for Hispanics, but impotent in bringing salvation for Euroamericans. In the famous biblical parable of the sheep and the goats as recorded in the Gospel of Matthew (25:31-46), Jesus divides those destined for glory (the sheep) from those destined for damnation (the goats). The salvation of those with power and privilege is contingent upon how they treated those who were starving, thirsty, aliens, unclothed, ill, and imprisoned. Usually, Hispanics occupy this space. The dominant culture finds its life (salvation) when it struggles alongside those who are oppressed by attempting to alleviate, if not eliminate, the structures that cause death. Crucial to the understanding of this passage is the radical revelation made by Jesus. He ends the parable by stating (v. 45), "Then [the Lord] will answer [the condemned], saying, 'Truly I say to you, inasmuch as you did not do for one of these, the least, neither did you do it for me.'" To "see" Jesus in U.S. history is to see him in God's crucified people, those oppressed by structural racism and ethnic discrimination.

20 Not only is the Latina/o Christ salvific for Hispanics, he is also salvific for Euroamericans. As Euroamericans attempt to base their theology and ethics on a "thick" Jesus, it is crucial to ask, who is this Jesus they want to thicken? If the answer is the same Eurocentric Christ of the dominant culture that is responsible for spiritually justifying much of the oppressive structures faced by Hispanics and other non-white groups, then Euroamericans are at risk of worshipping a false messiah with no ability to save or redeem them, or anyone else for that matter. For the sake of their own salvation, Euroamericans must put away their Euroamerican Christ, whether he be "thin" or "thick," and learn to walk in solidarity with the Christ of the oppressed and the people with whom Christ identified in the parable of the sheep and the goats.

21   For a detailed understanding of the development of the concept of Hispanic-based praxis, see Fernando Cascante-Gómez, "Ortho-praxis" (2009a: 689–98).

22   See the encyclicals *Gaudium et Spes* and *Octogesima Adveniens*.

CHAPTER 4

1   For a detailed understanding of the Young Lords, see Elias Ortega-Aponte, "Young Lords Party" (2009a: 583–85).

2   The Young Patriots was an organization comprised of poor whites living in the Chicago area.

3   Although the word *raza* is usually translated as "race," it connotes a sense of the Latino/a people or community.

4   For a detailed understanding of *Católicos por la Raza*, see Miguel A. De La Torre, "*Católicos por la Raza*" (2009a: 443) and Mario T. García, *Católicos* (2008: 131–70).

5   For a detailed understanding of the Riverside Manifesto, see Edwin D. Aponte, "Riverside Manifesto" (2009a: 661).

6   In his book *Rules for Radicals*, Alinsky provides examples of praxis planned by the marginalized that truly capture the spirit of *jodiendo*. To protest the establishment of the city of Rochester, he suggested purchasing one hundred tickets to a concert of the Rochester Symphony Orchestra. Prior to attending the event, the protestors would enjoy a preconcert dinner of nothing but baked beans. Once the concert began, they would let rip, bringing the concert to an end after the first movement. The establishment and police would be paralyzed to act, because there is no law against public flatulence. This praxis of *jodiendo* is designed to force the establishment to the negotiating table lest the dispossessed plan a repeat performance (1971: 139–40). Another example given in the book dealt with trying to get the Chicago Woodlawn Organization to negotiate with economically depressed black neighborhoods. The disenfranchised targeted O'Hare Airport. In the days when airport security was more relaxed, when anyone could walk up to the gates, they planned to occupy every restroom toilet and have four- and five-deep lines at all the urinals. This "shit-in" was designed to disrupt the airport by preventing those leaving their planes in desperate need of relieving themselves from doing so. When the tactic was purposely leaked, Woodlawn Organization came to the negotiating table prior to the planned event (1971: 142–44). A final example would illustrate the point of *jodiendo*. A high-end department store that refused to hire African Americans was targeted by the black community. They planned to have close to 3,000 African Americans, in their Sunday best, go shopping at the store on its busiest day—Saturday. They would spend all day questioning the sales staff on the quality of the merchandise before purchasing anything. Playing off of white fear, they would more than

likely scare off the regular white shoppers who would enter the store. In the last hour before closing they would purchase items C.O.D. (again, this was the late 1960s, before credit cards). This would further run up the cost to the store in overtime needed to process the rush of orders. When the items were delivered, they would refuse them, sending them back to the store, running up the store's delivery costs. Once the plans were disclosed by a known informant within the planning stage, the department store called for a meeting with the protest organizers to inform them that they were opening 186 new positions. For the first time, the department store had blacks working on the sales floor and in executive training (1971: 146–48).

7   Based on the 2000 U.S. census, Latino/as comprised 12.5% of the population, of which 43% lived in majority-Hispanic neighborhoods. The economic link to spatial segregation cannot go unnoticed. As Hispanic immigration has increased in the last thirty to forty years, there has been a 32% "residential separation of high-income Americans" from all other Americans—further draining Latino/a neighborhoods and others of capital and investment (Taylor and Morin, 2008: 9). Furthermore, according to a 2002 study from the Lewis Mumford Center for Comparative Urban and Regional Research, titled "Separate and Unequal: Racial and Ethnic Neighborhoods in the 21st Century and Sortable Lists of Population Data for Hispanic National-Origin Groups," Hispanics, like African Americans, live in neighborhoods with lower than average median household incomes and higher rates of poverty than the neighborhoods of Euroamericans and Asian Americans. Even higher-income Latina/os also dwell in neighborhoods characterized by lower levels of human capital. In addition, Hispanics are more than likely to live in overcrowded households—26% in 2003, compared to 4% of non-Hispanic whites or 8% of blacks (Diaz McConnell, 2008: 90).

8   Ronald Weitzer and Steven A. Tuch's recent study points to Latina/os' "disproportionate experience" of "police abuse" (in comparison to non-Hispanic whites). Their findings suggest that Latino/as, both personally and vicariously, are two to three times as likely as non-Hispanic whites to experience unjustifiable stops, insulting language, excessive force, or corrupt activities by police—this proportion holds true for repeated experiences as well—especially verbal abuse, excessive force, and unjustifiable stops (2004: 315–16).

9   Latino/as are three times as likely as non-Hispanic whites to be victims of a homicide and 1.6 times as likely to be victims of aggravated assault. Additionally Hispanics are 1.7 times as likely to be victims of a robbery (Martínez, 2008: 114, 116).

10   The jobless claim figures for August 2009 showed that the unemployment rate for Hispanics rose to 13.0%, compared to a non-Hispanic white unemployment rate of 8.9% and a national unemployment rate

of 9.7%. Note this figure does not include any undocumented unemployed workers or people "who have stopped looking" (U.S. Bureau of Labor Statistics, 2009: 1, 5–6).

11   Hispanics experience low socioeconomic status. In 2002, 27% of Hispanics 25 years or older failed to complete ninth grade—compared to 4% of non-Hispanic whites (Acevedo-Garcia and Bates, 2008: 102). A 2003 study conducted by the National Center for Educational Statistics, titled "The Condition of Education," showed that in 2001, Hispanics 16–24 years of age had a 27% high school dropout rate—compared to non-Hispanic whites at 7.3% (Vélez, 2008: 136). Additionally, a 2005 U.S. Department of Education report indicated that the need for physical school facility "repairs, though widespread, was distributed unequally throughout the nation: the greatest needs were in central cities, the West, large schools, secondary schools, schools where more than half of the students belong to racial/ethnic minorities, and schools where 70 percent or more of the students were poor." The estimated cost of repairs stood at $223 billion dollars. Furthermore, the report indicated that 25% or more of schools experience overcrowding in classrooms and use of portable buildings, both of which can harm classroom instruction, and their conditions were more common in schools with minority populations over 50% than in schools with smaller minority populations (Chaney and Lewis, 2007: 1, 7, 9, 14–16).

12   In general, Hispanics have higher poverty rates and lower income levels than non-Hispanic whites. In 2000, more than 20% of Latina/os lived below the poverty line—compared to 7.6% of non-Hispanic whites. Additionally, the household median income of non-Hispanic whites was over a third greater than that of Latina/os (Dávila, Mora, and Hales, 2008: 181). By 2006, according to the U.S. Census Bureau, Hispanic males' (all origins) median income for full-time, year-round work was $26,769, and that of Hispanic females was $24,214—compared to a median income of $41,386 for all males and $31,858 for all females in the general U.S. population. The report further stated that the percent of all Hispanics below the poverty line that year grew to 21.8%, compared to 12.6% for the general population (U.S. Bureau of the Census, 2006: 22–23). Additionally, according to U.S. census numbers released in September 2009, Hispanics bore the brunt of the recent recession, experiencing the biggest poverty rate jump among all ethnic and racial groups, from 21.5% to 23.2%. Latino/a children, who comprise 22% of all children in the nation, are worse off, with 30.3% of them living in poverty. And these numbers are increasing. For every 100 children who slipped into poverty during 2008, 71 were Hispanics. See William H. Frey, "The New Republic: Minorities Hit with Poverty Increase," *NPR News*, September 14, 2009.

13   In 2003, almost 10% of all Hispanic households—compared to 4%

of non-Hispanic white households—lived in moderately or severely inadequate housing, dwellings that lacked a complete kitchen, plumbing, or electricity, and/or had rodent activity. And yet, according to a 2005 report by the U.S. Bureau of Labor Statistics, Hispanics paid more for shelter, about 33% of their pretax income in 2003, compared to 26% by non-Hispanics (Diaz McConnell, 2008: 90).

14   A recent study indicated that 1 in 27 Hispanics is now incarcerated, compared to 1 in 45 non-Hispanic whites. States' funding for corrections has increased over 303% in the last twenty years, outpacing every other budgetary item except Medicaid (Warren, 2009: 7). According to a report published by the Justice Policy Institute, more than two-thirds of the budget of the Office of National Drug Control is used for decreasing the supply of drugs on the street, while only a third is used to fund treatment and prevention programs. Moreover, because of disparate economic factors and greater access to health care, non-Hispanic white rates of admission to substance abuse programs are double their drug incarceration rate, despite rates of drug use similar to those of other groups. The report also indicates that 16% of all people imprisoned suffer from serious mental problems; for lack of treatment, these mentally ill people are swept into the criminal justice system—blacks and Hispanics proportinately more than whites (Petteruti and Walsh, 2008: 21–22).

15   Hispanics are three times as likely as the general population to lack a regular health care provider. Statistically, "more than one-fourth of Hispanic adults in the United States lack a usual healthcare provider and a similar proportion report obtaining no health care information from medical personnel in the past year" (Livingston, Minushkin, and Cohn, 2008: 4–5). Moreover, the 2009 report *Income, Poverty, and Health Insurance Coverage in the United States: 2008*, by the U.S. Census Bureau, indicates that 30.7% of Hispanics remain uninsured, compared to only 10.8% of non-Hispanic whites. The rate of uninsured Hispanic children was 17.2%, compared to 6.7% for non-Hispanic white children (DeNavas-Walt, Proctor, and Smith, 2009: 26, 28).

16   According to the U.S. Census Bureau's "U.S. and World Population Clocks," the U.S. population stood at 307,579,441, or 4.53% of the world's population (6,787,342,395). See http://www.census .gov/main/www/popclock.html (accessed on September 29, 2009). Having less than 5% of the world's population, in 2008 the U.S. consumed 19,497,964 barrels of oil per day, or 22.7% of world consumption (85,777,270 barrels per day). Latin America, on the other hand, uses 7,602,465 barrels per day, and Africa 3,235,000 barrels per day. See http://tonto.eia.doe.gov/cfapps/ipdbproject/IEDIndex3 .cfm?tid=5&pid=54&aid=2 (accessed on September 29, 2009). Total primary energy consumption for the U.S. in 2006 was 99.889 Q. BTUs (quadrillion BTUs), or 21.16% of the total world consumption

(472.078 Q. BTUs); Latin America, 24.231 Q. BTUs; Africa, 14.504 Q. BTUs. See http://tonto.eia.doe.gov/cfapps/ipdbproject/IEDIndex3.cfm?tid=44&pid=44&aid=2 (accessed on September 29, 2009).

17   "Act only on that maxim whereby thou canst at the same time will that it should become a universal law" (Kant, 1785 [2008]: 39).

18   According to a report recently released by the Civil Rights Project of UCLA, "Segregated black and Latino schools have less prepared teachers and classmates, and lower achievement and graduation." The Supreme Court heard and decided the voluntary integration case *Parents Involved in Community Schools (PICS) v. Seattle School Districts, 127 S. Ct. 2738* in 2007. That decision outlawed very widely used forms of voluntary integration by school districts not under court order, districts that wished to foster integrated education. As a result "we now have a society where 44 percent of our public school children are non-white and our two largest minority populations, Latinos and African Americans, are more segregated than they have been since the death of Martin Luther King more than forty years ago." In fact, 40% of Latino/as attend a school comprised of a 90%–100% minority (non-white) population. Latinos also had the least contact with non-Hispanic whites: "on average Latinos had only 27% white fellow students, while many schools were vastly more segregated." Finally, Hispanic children were in schools in which 57.4% of the students lived in poverty in 2006–2007, compared to a rate of 31.5% for white children (Orfield, 2009: 6, 8, 12–14).

19   Even though 3,000 of the 3,141 counties in the U.S. have experienced Hispanic population growth, "at the same time, Hispanic population growth in the new century has been fairly concentrated. Hispanic population growth in just 178 counties accounts for 79% of the nation's entire 10.2 million Hispanic population increase." Furthermore, "in spite of the geographic dispersal of Hispanics, the Hispanic population continues to be much more geographically concentrated than the non-Hispanic population. In 2007 the 100 largest Hispanic counties were home to 73% of the Latino population. By contrast, the 100 largest non-Hispanic counties were home to just 39% of the nation's non-Hispanics." By this measure, Hispanics are more geographically concentrated than the nation's black population. Nearly six in ten (59%) members of the non-Hispanic black population live in the nation's 100 largest non-Hispanic black counties (Fry, 2008: 4).

20   Within the U.S. labor force, Latino/as "are overrepresented in low-wage jobs with low requirements for education and experience." Latino/as comprise 14% of employed adults, yet they represent 20.2% of employees in the service sector. Using Toussaint-Comeau's socioeconomic index score, which measures wages and human capital requirements, such as education, "more than half of the Latino

workforce is employed in the eight major occupation groups with the lowest socioeconomic index scores: farming, fishing, and forestry; food preparation and service; building/grounds cleaning and maintenance; personal care and service; health care support; transportation and material moving; production; and construction and extraction" (Singley, 2009: 7–9). Accordingly, the U.S. Department of Commerce reports that 24% percent of Hispanics aged 16 and older worked in service occupations; 16% in construction, extraction, and maintenance occupations; and approximately 19% in production, transportation, and material moving occupations compared to 14%, 10%, and 12% for non-Hispanic whites, respectively. Furthermore, about 38% of non-Hispanic whites worked in managerial, professional, and related occupations; and about 27% worked in sales and office occupations. Hispanics were less likely to work in these occupations, with about 18% in managerial, professional, and related occupations; and about 22% worked in sales and office occupations (2007: 16).

21   It is important to note that the overwhelming majority of trickster figures are portrayed as male, even though trickery and deceit are not limited to one gender. No doubt a historical and/or cultural sexist implication might be that women, as female tricksters, are unable to outwit others.

22   I am grateful to Edwin D. Aponte Alain Silverio, and Manuel A. Vásquez for enlightening me on several trickster figures, some of which are included in this section.

23   *Quwi* is the Quechua word for guinea pig; in Spanish the word is *cuy*.

24   The stage name of Mario Moreno Reyes (1911–1993), who made over fifty feature films, two in Hollywood: *Around the World in Eighty Days* and *Pepe.*

25   Started by Luis Miguel Valdez in 1965 during the United Farm Workers grape strike, *El Teatro Campesino* assisted the union in organizing and raising the consciousness of farm workers. The actors were striking farm workers who wrote skits that conveyed the union's message.

26   It is important to note that Albert Hernandez and I are in the process of completing a book for Fortress Press titled *The Quest for the Historical Satan* (2011), whose major thesis is a call to move beyond the concept of Satan as signifying ultimate evil and toward a conception of him as signifying the trickster figure.

27   I am grateful to John Fife, pastor emeritus of Southside Presbyterian Church, who taught me this concept while we were providing food and medical attention to the undocumented walking the migrant trails. Rev. Fife is a cofounder of No More Deaths and an active volunteer in that movement. He was also one of the founding members of the Sanctuary Movement of the 1980s.

WORKS CITED

Acevedo-Garcia, Dolores, and Lisa M. Bates. 2008. "Latino Health Paradoxes: Empirical Evidence, Explanations, Future Research, and Implications." In H. Rodríguez et al., *Latinas/os in the United States.*

Albrecht, Gloria. 1995. *The Character of Our Communities: Toward an Ethic of Liberation for the Church.* Nashville: Abingdon.

Alinsky, Saul D. 1971. *Rules for Radicals: A Pragmatic Primer for Realistic Radicals.* New York: Vintage.

Alumkal, Antony W. 2004. "American Evangelicalism in the Post-Civil Rights Era: A Racial Formation Theory Analysis." *Sociology of Religion* 65.3: 195–213.

Aponte, Edwin D. 2009a. "Riverside Manifesto." In De La Torre, *Encyclopedia.*

Aquino, María Pilar. 1993. *Our Cry for Life: Feminist Theology from Latin America.* Maryknoll, N.Y.: Orbis.

Bentham, Jeremy. 1787 [1843]. "Panopticon, or The Inspection-House, & C." In *The Works of Jeremy Bentham.* Vol. 4. Edited by John Bowing. Edinburgh: William Tait, Prince St.

Bonino, José Míguez. 1983. *Toward a Christian Political Ethics.* Philadelphia: Fortress.

Campolo, Anthony, Jr. 1984. *The Power Delusion.* Wheaton, Ill.: Victor.

———. 1985. *We Have Met the Enemy, and They Are Partly Right.* Waco, Tex.: Jarrell Binding.

———. 1991. *Wake Up, America! Answering God's Radical Call While Living in the Real World.* New York: HarperCollins

———. 1992. *How to Rescue the Earth without Worshiping Nature.* Nashville: Thomas Nelson.

———. 1997. *Following Jesus without Embarrassing God.* Dallas: Word.

———. 2000a. *Let Me Tell You a Story.* Nashville: Word.

————. 2000b. *Revolution and Renewal: How Churches Are Saving Our Cities*. Louisville: Westminster John Knox.

————. 2003. "Missing the Point: Social Action." In *Adventures in Missing the Point: How the Culture-Controlled Church Neutered the Gospel*. Edited by Brian D. McLaren and Anthony Campolo. Grand Rapids: Zondervan.

Campolo, Anthony, Jr., and Gordon Aeschliman. 2006. *Everybody Wants to Change the World: Practical Ideas for Social Justice*. Ventura, Calif.: Regal.

Cascante-Gómez, Fernando. 2009a. "Orthopraxis." In De La Torre, *Encyclopedia*.

Chaney, Bradford, and Laurie Lewis. 2007. *Public School Principals Report on Their School Facilities: Fall 2005*. Washington, D.C.: National Center for Educational Statistics, U.S. Department of Education.

Chomsky, Noam, and Edward S. Herman. 1979. *The Political Economy of Human Rights: The Washington Connection and Third World Fascism*. Boston: South End.

Dávila, Alberto, Marie T. Mora, and Alma D. Hales. 2008. "Income, Earnings, and Poverty: A Portrait of Inequality among Latinos/as in the United States." In H. Rodríguez et al., *Latinas/os in the United States*.

De La Torre, Miguel A. 2002. *Reading the Bible from the Margins*. Maryknoll, N.Y.: Orbis.

————. 2004. *Doing Christian Ethics from the Margins*. Maryknoll, N.Y.: Orbis.

————. 2007. *Liberating Jonah: Forming an Ethics of Reconciliation*. Maryknoll, N.Y.: Orbis.

————, ed. 2009a. *Encyclopedia on Hispanic American Religious Culture*. Santa Barbara, Calif.: ABC-CLIO.

————. 2009a. "Católicos por la Ráza." In De La Torre, *Encyclopedia*.

————. 2009a. "Introduction." In De La Torre, *Encyclopedia*.

————. 2009b. *Trails of Hope and Terror: Testimonies on Immigration*. Maryknoll, N.Y.: Orbis.

DeNavas-Walt, Carmen, Bernadette D. Proctor, and Jessica C. Smith. 2009. *Income, Poverty, and Health Insurance Coverage in the United States: 2008*. Current Population Reports P60-236. Washington, D.C.: U.S. Census Bureau.

Diaz McConnell, Eileen. 2008. "U.S. Latinos/as and the 'American Dream': Diverse Populations and Unique Challenges in Housing." In H. Rodríguez et al., *Latinas/os in the United States*.

Dirks, Nicholas. 1989. "Castes of Mind." *Representations*, no. 37. Edited by Svetlana Alpers, Stephen Greenblatt, et al. Berkeley: University of California Press.

Dorrien, Gary. 2003. *The Making of American Liberal Theology: Idealism,*

Realism, & Modernity, 1900–1950. Louisville: Westminster John Knox.

Ehrenreich, Barbara. 2001. *Nickel and Dimed: On (Not) Getting By in America.* New York: Holt.

Elizondo, Virgilio. 1983. *Galilean Journey: The Mexican-American Promise.* Maryknoll, N.Y.: Orbis.

Evans, Christopher H. 2009. *The Kingdom Is Always but Coming: A Life of Walter Rauschenbusch.* Waco, Tex.: Baylor University Press.

Fife, John. 2009. "Civil Initiative." In *Trails of Hope and Terror: Testimonies on Immigration.* Edited by Miguel A. De La Torre. Maryknoll, N.Y.: Orbis.

Foucault, Michel. 1978. *The History of Sexuality.* Vol. 1: *An Introduction.* Translated by Robert Hurley. New York: Vintage.

———. 1984. *The Foucault Reader.* Edited by Paul Rabinow. New York: Pantheon.

———. 1995. *Discipline and Punish: The Birth of the Prison.* Translated by Alan Sheridan. New York: Vintage.

Fry, Richard. 2008. *Latino Settlement in the New Century.* Washington, D.C.: Pew Hispanic Center.

García, Ismael. 1997. *Dignidad: Ethics through Hispanic Eyes.* Nashville: Abingdon.

———. 2009a. "Ethics." In De La Torre, *Encyclopedia.*

García, Mario T. 2008. *Católicos: Resistance and Affirmation in Chicano Catholic History.* Austin: University of Texas Press.

Goizueta, Roberto S. 1995. *Caminemos con Jesús: Toward a Hispanic/ Latino Theology of Accompaniment.* Maryknoll, N.Y.: Orbis.

———. 2009a. "Acompañado." In De La Torre, *Encyclopedia.*

González, Justo L. 1990. *Mañana: Christian Theology from a Hispanic Perspective.* Nashville: Abingdon.

Gushee, David. 2008. *The Future of Faith in American Politics: The Public Witness of the Evangelical Center.* Waco, Tex.: Baylor University Press.

Gustafson, James M. 1975. *Can Ethics Be Christian?* Chicago: University of Chicago Press.

———. 1985. "The Sectarian Temptation: Reflections on Theology, the Church and the University." In *Proceedings of the Catholic Theological Society* 40: 83–94.

Harlow, Caroline Wolf. 2003. *Education and Correctional Populations.* Washington, D.C.: Bureau of Justice Statistics, U.S. Department of Justice.

Hauerwas, Stanley. 1974. *Vision and Virtue: Essays in Christian Ethical Reflection.* Notre Dame, Ind.: Fides.

———. 1975. *Character and the Christian Life: A Study in Theological Ethics.* San Antonio: Trinity University Press.

————. 1977. "Learning to See Red Wheelbarrows: On Vision and Relativism." *Journal of the American Academy of Religion* 45: 643–55.

————. 1981. *A Community of Character: Toward a Constructive Christian Social Ethics.* Notre Dame, Ind.: University of Notre Dame Press.

————. 1983. *The Peaceable Kingdom: A Primer in Christian Ethics.* Notre Dame, Ind.: University of Notre Dame Press.

————. 1985. "The Gesture of a Truthful Story." *Theology Today* 42.2: 181–89.

————. 1986. "Some Theological Reflections on Gutiérrez's Use of 'Liberation' as a Theological Concept," *Modern Theology* 3.1: 67–76.

————. 1988. "Taking Time for Peace: The Ethical Significance of the Trivial." In *Christian Existence Today: Essays on Church, World, and Living in Between.* Durham: Labyrinth.

————. 1991. *After Christendom? How the Church Is to Behave if Freedom, Justice, and a Christian Nation Are Bad Ideas.* Nashville: Abingdon.

————. 1997. *Wilderness Wanderings: Probing Twentieth-Century Theology and Philosophy.* Boulder, Colo.: Westview.

————. 2000. *A Better Hope: Resources for a Church Confronting Capitalism, Democracy, and Postmodernity.* Grand Rapids: Brazos.

————. 2004. *Performing the Faith: Bonhoeffer and the Practice of Nonviolence.* Grand Rapids: Brazos.

Isasi-Díaz, Ada María. 1993. *En la Lucha, in the Struggle: A Hispanic Women's Liberation Theology.* Philadelphia: Fortress.

————. 2009a. "la Lucha." In De La Torre, *Encyclopedia.*

Kant, Immanuel. 1785 [2008]. *Groundwork of the Metaphysics of Morals.* Radford, Va.: Wilder.

King, Martin Luther, Jr. 1964. "Letter from Birmingham Jail." In *Why We Can't Wait.* New York: Mentor.

Klor de Alva, J. Jorge. 1982. "Spiritual Conflict and Accommodation in New Spain: Toward a Typology of Aztec Response to Christianity." In *The Inca and Aztec States, 1400–1800: Anthropology and History.* Edited by George A. Collier, I. Rosaldo Renato, and D. Wirth John. New York: Academic.

Lamy, Philip. 1996. *Millennium Rage: Survivalists, White Supremacists, and the Doomsday Prophecy.* New York: Plenum.

Livingston, Gretchen, Susan Minushkin, and D'Vera Cohn. 2008. *Hispanics and Health Care in the United States: Access, Information and Knowledge.* Washington, D.C.: Pew Hispanic Center.

Lovin, Robin W. 2000. *Christian Ethics: An Essential Guide.* Nashville: Abingdon.

Martínez, Ramiro, Jr. 2008. "Latino Crime and Delinquency in the United States." In H. Rodríguez et al., *Latinas/os in the United States.*

Medina, Lara. 2009a. "Nepantla." In De La Torre, *Encyclopedia.*

Nanko-Fernández, Carmen M. 2009a. "Cotidiano, lo." In De La Torre, *Encyclopedia.*

National Council of La Raza. 2009. *Arrested Development: Foreclosures Eroding the Latino Community.* Fact Sheet. Washington, D.C.: National Council of La Raza.

Niebuhr, Reinhold. 1928. "The Confession of a Tired Radical." *Christian Century,* August 30: 1046–47.

———. 1932. *Moral Man and Immoral Society: A Study in Ethics and Politics.* New York: Scribner.

———. 1941. *The Nature and Destiny of Man.* New York: Scribner.

———. 1942. "Plans for World Reorganization." In *Christianity and Crisis* 2.17: 3–6.

———. 1943. "Anglo-Saxon Destiny and Responsibility." *Christianity and Crisis* 3.16: 2–3.

———. 1952. *The Irony of American History.* New York: Scribner.

———. 1959. *The Structure of Nations and Empires: A Study of the Recurring Patterns and Problems of the Political Order in Relationship to the Unique Problems of the Nuclear Age.* New York: Scribner.

———. 1961. "Well-Tempered Evangelism," *New Republic,* June 26: 11–12.

———. 1962a. "The Alternatives to Communism," *New Republic,* October 1: 15–16.

———. 1962b. "American Hegemony and the Prospects for Peace." *Annals of the American Academy of Political and Social Science* 342.1: 154–60.

Orfield, Gary. 2009. *Reviving the Goal of an Integrated Society: A 21st Century Challenge.* Los Angeles: The Civil Rights Project at UCLA.

Ortega-Aponte, Elias. 2009a. "Young Lords Party." In De La Torre, *Encyclopedia.*

Park, Andrew Sung. 1998. *Racial Conflict and Healing: An Asian-American Theological Perspective.* Maryknoll, N.Y.: Orbis.

Pedraja, Luis G. 2009a. "Christology." In De La Torre, *Encyclopedia.*

Petteruti, Amanda, and Natassia Walsh. 2008. *Moving Target: A Decade of Resistance to the Prison Industrial Complex.* Washington, D.C.: Justice Policy Institute.

Ramsey, Paul. 1961. *Christian Ethics and the Sit-In.* New York: Association.

Rauschenbusch, Walter. 1881 [2009]. "My Country." Cited in Evans, *The Kingdom Is Always but Coming.*

———. 1896. "The Ideals of Social Reformers." *American Journal of Sociology* 2, no. 2: 202–19.

———. 1898 [2009]. "The Present and the Future." Cited in Evans, *The Kingdom Is Always but Coming.*

———. 1902. "The Contribution of Germany to the National Life of

America." Commencement address to Rochester Theological Seminary. Cited in Vinz, *Pulpit Politics*.

———. 1907 [1991]. *Christianity and the Social Crisis*. Louisville: Westminster John Knox.

———. 1911. "The Church and Social Questions." *Conservation of National Ideals*. New York: Revell.

———. 1912 [2009]. *Christianizing the Social Order*. Waco, Tex.: Baylor University Press.

———. 1917. *A Theology for the Social Gospel*. Nashville: Abingdon.

Rawls, John. 1971. *A Theory of Justice*. Cambridge, Mass.: Belknap Press of Harvard University Press.

Rodríguez, Havidán, Rogelio Sáenz, and Cecilia Menjívar, eds. 2008. *Latinas/os in the United States: Changing the Face of America*. New York: Springer.

Rodríguez, José David, and Loida I. Martell-Otero, eds. 1997. *Teología en Conjunto: A Collaborative Hispanic Protestant Theology*. Louisville: Westminster John Knox.

Rodríguez-Díaz, Daniel R. 2009a. "Teología en Conjunto." In De La Torre, *Encyclopedia*.

Said, Edward W. 1979. *Orientalism*. New York: Vintage.

Scott, James C. 1990. *Domination and the Arts of Resistance*. New Haven: Yale University Press.

Sider, Ronald J. 1980. "An Evangelical Theology of Liberation." *Christian Century*, March 19: 314–18.

———. 1993. *One-Sided Christianity: Uniting the Church to Heal a Lost and Broken World*. Grand Rapids: Zondervan.

———. 1997. *Rich Christians in an Age of Hunger: Moving from Affluence to Generosity*. Rev. ed. Nashville: Word.

———. 1999. *Just Generosity: A New Vision for Overcoming Poverty in America*. Grand Rapids: Baker.

Singley, Catherine. 2009. *Fractures in the Foundation: The Latino Worker's Experience in an Era of Declining Job Quality*. Washington, D.C.: The National Council of La Raza.

Smith, Christian. 1991. *The Emergence of Liberation Theology: Radical Religion and Social Movement Theology*. Chicago: University of Chicago Press.

Smith, Robert F. 1963. *What Happened in Cuba? A Documentary History*. New York: Twayne.

Taylor, Paul, and Richard Morin. 2008. *Americans Say They Like Diverse Communities; Election, Census Trends Suggest Otherwise*. Washington, D.C.: Pew Research Center.

Thistlethwaite, Susan Brooks. 2003. "Introduction: Liberation Theology in Dialogue with the Human Genome Project." In *Adam, Eve, and the*

Genome: The Human Genome Project and Theology. Edited by Susan Brooks Thistlethwaite. Minneapolis: Fortress.

Thomson, John B. 2003. *The Ecclesiology of Stanley Hauerwas: A Christian Theology of Liberation.* Burlington, Vt.: Ashgate.

Turner, Victor W. 1969. *The Ritual Process: Structure and Anti-Structure.* Chicago: Aldine.

U.S. Bureau of Labor Statistics. 2009. *The Employment Situation–August 2009.* News Release. USDL-09-1067. Washington, D.C.: U.S. Department of Labor.

U.S. Bureau of the Census. 2006. "Population Size and Composition." In *U.S. Hispanic Population: 2006.* Washington, D.C.: prepared by the Ethnicity and Ancestry Statistics Branch of the Population Division, Bureau of the Census.

———. 2007. *The American Community—Hispanics: 2004.* American Community Survey Reports 3. Washington, D.C. prepared by the Ethnicity and Ancestry Branch, Bureau of the Census. Washington, D.C.

Vélez, William. 2008. "The Education Experiences of Latinos in the United States." In H. Rodríguez et al., *Latinas/os in the United States.*

Vinz, Warren L. 1989. *Pulpit Politics: Faces of American Protestant Nationalism in the Twentieth Century.* Albany: State University of New York Press.

Villafañe, Eldin. 1993. *The Liberating Spirit: Toward an Hispanic American Pentecostal Social Ethic.* Grand Rapids: Eerdmans.

Walker, Nancy E., J. Michael Senger, Francisco A. Villarruel, and Angela M. Arboleda. 2004. *Lost Opportunities: The Reality of Latinos in the U.S. Criminal Justice System.* Washington, D.C.: National Council of La Raza.

Wallis, Jim. 1976. *Agenda for Biblical People.* New York: Harper.

———. 2005. *God's Politics: Why the Right Gets It Wrong and the Left Doesn't Get It.* New York: HarperCollins.

Warren, Jenifer. 2009. *One in 31: The Long Reach of American Corrections.* Washington, D.C.: The Pew Center on the States.

Weitzer, Ronald, and Steven A. Tuch. 2004. "Race and Perceptions of Police Misconduct." *Social Problems* 51.3: 305–25.

West, Traci C. 2006. *Disruptive Christian Ethics: When Racism and Women's Lives Matter.* Louisville: Westminster John Knox.

Winant, Howard. 2004. *The New Politics of Race: Globalism, Difference, Justice.* Minneapolis: University of Minnesota Press.

Wogaman, J. Philip. 2000. *Christian Perspectives on Politics.* Louisville: Westminster John Knox.

INDEX

Abimelech of Gerar, King, 114
Abraham, patriarch, 94, 114
academy and academics, ix–xi, 3,
    30–31, 36, 42–43, 67–69, 87–88,
    96, 131n9, 132nn10, 16, 136n11;
    Euroamerican, ix, 3, 31, 67–69,
    71, 75, 80, 88; Hispanic, 11, 59,
    61–62, 67–71, 73, 87, 94, 96,
    131n9, 132n10
Achish of Gath, King, 115
acompañamiento, 77–78, 80, 87–88,
    133n17
Adrian Sisters Order, 51
Aeschliman, Gordon, 49
affirmative action, 38, 132n16
AFL-CIO, 52
Africa, 13, 137n16
African Americans, 7–8, 16–17,
    46, 49, 53, 56–59, 61, 91, 119,
    126n1, 128n12, 134n6, 135n7,
    137n14, 138nn18–19; Black
    Panthers, 90
Agenda for Biblical People, 55
Albrecht, Gloria, 127n9
Alicea, Benjamin, 96
Alinsky, Saul, 93–94, 98, 134n6
Alliance for Progress, 49
Alumkal, Antony, 38
American Mission Association, 7

Andes, 109
Anglo-Saxons, 8, 13, 15
Aquino, María Pilar, 68, 70
Arizona, 73, 80
Arminius, 8
Arroyo, Dolly, 130n31
Aryan Nation, 37
Asian Americans, 8, 16, 53,
    126nn1, 3, 135n7
Assyria, 11
Augustine of Hippo, 18, 97
Augustus, emperor, 12
Austin Presbyterian Theological
    Seminary, 131n1

Banks, Michael and Addie, 128n12
barrios, 60, 71, 78, 80–81, 89, 90,
    95, 98–100, 103, 132n16, 135n7,
    136n13
Bauer, Gary, 38
Belgium, 12
Bentham, Jeremy, 102
Bible, 4, 11, 23, 27, 43–48, 54–55,
    67, 76–77, 81–87, 94, 97, 114–16,
    119, 125n1, 127n9, 129n14; Gos-
    pels, ix, 4, 7, 18, 21, 35, 43–44,
    47, 75, 77, 81–82, 86, 92, 97, 106,
    133n19
Birmingham, Ala., 40

borders and borderlands, 29–30,
　35, 72–74, 76, 79, 100–101, 103,
　107, 119–21
Bosch, Juan, 52
Boston University, 131n2
Brown, Tim, 128n12
Buchanan, Patrick, 33, 37, 128n1
Buddhism, 54
Bush, George W., 35–36, 42, 56
Bush Sr., George, 37

Caldwell, Kirbyjon, 129n
California, 37, 61, 73, 117
Call to Renewal, 55
Camara, Helder, 60, 129n28
Campolo, Anthony, 36, 42, 48–54,
　56, 59–60, 128n10
Candomble, 108
Cantinflas, 112–13, 139n24
capitalism, 12, 20, 29, 36, 39, 45,
　49–51, 58, 98, 110, 135n7; *see
　also* neoliberalism
Caribbean, 21, 108; *see also* Latin
　America
Carter, Jimmy, 55–56
caste system, 44, 128n11
Castro, Fidel, 110
categorical imperative, 28, 99,
　128n13, 138n17
Catholicism, 10, 85, 95, 100, 117,
　134n4
Católicos por la Raza, 95, 134n4
Central America, 13, 21, 30, 60,
　119; *see also* Latin America
Changó, 109
Chávez, César, 60, 117, 130n31
Chicago, Ill., 89–90
Chicago Woodlawn Organization,
　134n6
China, 18
Christian Identity, 37
Christianity and the Social Crisis, 11
Chula Vista, Calif., 73
church (ecclesiology), 6–7, 10,
　12–13, 21, 27, 41, 47, 49, 68,

78, 80–81, 83, 90–91, 95–96,
　100–101, 113, 116–17, 119, 122,
　127nn9, 11, 139n27; liturgy, 24,
　80, 95–96, 133n20; megachurch,
　42, 129n25
civil disobedience, 26, 92, 97,
　119–20
civil initiative, 92, 97, 118–21
civil rights, 16–17, 38
Civil Rights Project of UCLA,
　138n18
Civil War, 6
classism, 3–4, 14–15, 20, 26, 29,
　36, 44, 73, 83, 126n5, 131n5,
　132n16, 135n7, 136nn11–12,
　137n14, 138n20; middle-class
　privilege, 7–8, 14, 24, 26, 29,
　34–35, 46–47, 71, 93
Clinton, Bill, 48
Clinton, Hillary, 56–58
Coca-Cola, 41
Cold War, 15, 33
colonialism, 9, 11–12, 18–20,
　23–24, 43–46, 49, 57, 80–81, 83,
　110, 113, 126n5, 128n11; post-
　colonialism, 57, 131n5
color-blind, x, 37–38
communism, 15, 19–20, 55, 91, 110
comunidad, 35, 68–69, 73, 75–78,
　81, 83, 88, 99, 106, 108, 132n10
Cone, James, 59
Congo, 12
conjunto, en, 76–77, 83, 86–88,
　122, 132n15
conservatism, 4, 10, 15, 33, 34–35,
　38, 42–43, 46, 55, 63, 79, 96,
　116, 125n2, 129n25; *see also*
　neoconservatism
Coors, Joseph, 38
Corbett, Jim, 120
Costas, Olando E., 130n31
cotidiano, lo, 70–72, 74, 77, 86–88,
　107, 132n12
Cruz, Ricardo, 95
Cuba, 10, 110–11, 126n7, 131n3;

Cuban Americans, 53, 91, 103, 110, 126n7
Culiacan, Sinaloa, 118
cultural war, 33–36, 62
Custer, George Armstrong, 8
Cuy: *see* Quwi

David, King, 115
Deats, Paul K., 131n2
de Cervantes, Miguel, 112
De La Torre, Miguel A., 3, 67, 84, 126n7, 129n14, 131n5, 132n11, 139n26
DeLay, Tom, 38
Delilah, 115
democracy, 9, 14, 19, 49, 52, 57–58, 97, 101, 126n7
Democratic Party, 34, 42, 58, 102, 128n9
Dennis, James, 128n12
Detroit, Mich., 15
Dewey, George, 9
Dirks, Nicholas, 128n11
Division Street Riots, 89
Dobson, James, 36, 38
Doing Christian Ethics from the Margins, 84, 132n11
Domination and the Arts of Resistance, 106
Dominican Republic, 51–53; Dominican Americans, 53, 110
Don Cacahuate, 111–12
Dorrien, Gary, 126n1
double-consciousness, xi, 14
Douglas, Ariz., 73
Drew University, 131n3

Eastern University, 48, 50
East Harlem Garbage Offensive, 89
ecclesiology: *see* church
Eglon, King, 115
Egypt, 114–15
Ehrenreich, Barbara, 46
Ehud, 115
Elegguá: *see* Eshu

Elizondo, Virgilio, 68
El Paso, Tex., 73, 121
El Salvador, 119
empire, 12–13, 18–19, 30, 35, 38, 45, 48–49, 93, 98, 106, 114, 119, 122, 125n1; British, 44, 128n11; Roman, 12, 82, 125n2; Soviet, 18, 20–21; U.S., xii, 3–5, 9–13, 15, 17–21, 23, 26–27, 30–36, 38–41, 43–46, 48–60, 62–63, 79, 92–94, 97–98, 100–101, 107–8, 120, 122, 125n1, 126n7, 128n3
employment, 15, 51–52, 60–61, 71, 91, 95, 98, 103–4, 130n35, 135n10, 136n12, 138n20, 139n25
English only, 37, 60, 107
Enlightenment Project, 21, 127nn10–11
epistemological privilege, 14, 72
Esau, 114
eschatology, 25–26
Eshu, 108–9
ethics: abstract based, 4, 14, 17, 26–27, 30–31, 70, 75–76, 84, 99, 122, 127n12; aesthetics, 22, 70; autobiographical, 71, 77; contextual, 3, 5–6, 11, 20, 24, 27–28, 63, 68–71, 73, 75–76, 88, 131n2; economic, 36, 39, 51; empire, 4–5, 9, 20, 23, 26–27, 31–36, 43–46, 56, 62–63, 79, 94, 97, 100–101, 106, 108, 119; Eurocentric, ix–xii, 3–6, 9, 13–18, 20–22, 25–29, 30–32, 41, 43, 61–62, 67, 69–72, 75, 83–84, 87–88, 94, 96, 104, 100, 117–19, 133n20; Hispanic, x–xii, 4–6, 14, 28, 33, 35, 39–40, 43, 47–48, 62, 63, 67–88, 91–123; liberative, 7, 14, 17–18, 21, 23, 25, 31–32, 41, 47–48, 62–63, 70, 74–75, 92, 94, 97–98, 108, 118–19, 122; *para joder*, 92–99, 101, 105–6, 115, 119, 122–23; pastoral, 121–23; praxis oriented, 4, 43, 70, 78,

83–88; realism, 14; socialist based, 15; theological, 21–22; virtue (areteological), 21, 23, 26–30, 71, 83–84, 94, 97, 108, 110, 122
ethnic discrimination, ix–xii, 4–5, 15, 49, 57, 67, 75, 81–82, 98, 120, 132n19
evangelical, 38, 43–44, 46–48, 55, 84, 96
Evangelical Association for the Promotion of Education, 48
Evangelicals for Social Action, 43
Exodus, book of, 115
Exu: *see* Eshu

Falwell, Jerry, 36
Fanon, Frantz, 39
Fargo, N.D., 73
Federal Bureau of Investigation, 91
Fife, John, 139n27
Florida farm workers, 130n35
Foucault, Michel, 99, 102
Francis, St., 113
Fundamentalists, 96

Galilee, 82
Gallegos, Aaron, 61
García, Ismael, 4, 67, 131n1, 132n10
General Motors, 41
Genesis, book of, 114–15
Germany, 126n5; German Americans, 8–9, 126n1
Gibeonites, 115
God's Politics, 58
Goizueta, Roberto, 78
good/evil dualism, 28, 105–6, 114, 118
Good Neighbor Policy, 35, 49, 128n3
González, Justo, 68
Gordon-Conwell Theological Seminary, 131n2
Graduate Theological Union, 131n4
Granado, Lorraine, 130n33

Guam, 10
Guatemala, 119; Guatemalans, 110
Gulf and Western, 51–52
gunboat diplomacy, 21, 35, 49, 79, 128n3
Gunowners of America, 37
Gushee, David, 39, 56, 58, 128n10
Gustafson, James, 17, 26, 131n1
Gutiérrez, Gustavo, 25, 127n10

Habana, Cuba, 110–11
Harding, Vincent, 59
Harlem, N.Y., 89–90, 96
Harrison, Beverly, 131n3
Hauerwas, Stanley, xi, 5–6, 10, 13, 21–27, 32, 127nn8–12
health care, 43, 89, 91, 98, 104, 137nn14–15, 138n20
hermeneutical circle, 85–87, 119
Hernandez, Albert, 139n26
Hinduism, 27, 44
hope, 7–8, 24–25, 33–34, 39, 68, 78, 81, 92–94, 106
Horton, Willie, 37
hospitality, virtue of, 26–27
Houston, Tex., 128n2
human rights, 29–30, 35, 39, 89, 119–20
Hunter, Joel C., 129n25

IBM, 41
Iliff School of Theology, xii, 131n5
immigration, 8, 37, 82, 120, 128n9; Hispanic, 26–27, 29–30, 34–35, 37, 50, 53, 57–58, 60–61, 71, 80, 101, 103, 107, 118–21, 132n16, 135n7; Operation Gatekeeper, 35, 121
India, 18, 44, 128n11
industrialization, 6, 43, 51–52; *see also* capitalism
institutional violence, 25, 39, 63, 98, 103–4, 106, 118
Iowa, 34, 73
Iraq, 56

Isaac, patriarch, 114
Isasi-Díaz, Ada María, 67, 74–75, 130n33, 131n3, 132n10
Islam, 10, 12, 27

Jackson, Mich., 73
Jacob, patriarch, 114
Jael, 115
Jakes, Bishop T. D., 129n25
James, epistle of, 23, 84–85
Jefferson, Thomas, 45
Jerusalem, 82
Jesus Christ, ix, 9, 21–22, 24–26, 35, 38, 43–44, 46–48, 54–55, 62, 75, 78, 81–84, 115–17, 133nn18–20; a Euroamerican, 9, 46, 55, 79–81, 133nn19–20; a Hispanic 79–81
Jews, 12, 27, 37; anti-Semitic, 23
Jim and Jane Crow, 7, 120
Jiménez, José "Cha Cha", 89
jingoism, 10, 13, 126n4
Job, book of, 93
joder, an ethics *para*, 92–99, 101, 105–6, 115, 119, 122–23, 134n6
John, gospel of, 75, 77, 81, 106
John Paul II, Pope, 45
Juan Bobo, 111
Juan Diego, 113
Juárez Maso, Jesús: *see* Malverde, Jesús
Judges, book of, 115
justice, 4–5, 9, 12, 14, 17, 21, 27, 40–45, 47–48, 68, 86, 88, 93, 97–98, 101, 103–4, 106, 122, 125n2, 126n7, 127n12; biblical, 44–45, 97; economic, 36, 51; lack of, 15–16, 28–29, 44, 51, 53–54, 70, 74, 77, 97, 126n5; liberative, xii, 18, 22, 31, 46, 71, 73–74, 83, 97, 99, 123
Justice Policy Institute, 137n14

Kansas, 34
Kant, Immanuel, 28, 99, 127n10

kingdom (reign) of God, 6–7, 9, 21–23, 26, 47–48, 83
King Jr., Martin Luther, 25, 40, 119, 138n18
Klor de Alva, J. Jorge, 74
Klu Klux Klan, 37, 40–41
Korea, 19

Laban, 114
Latin America, 10, 13, 21, 27, 30, 51–53, 59–60, 72, 79, 90, 97, 100–11, 113, 117–21, 126n7, 128n3, 129n28, 130n31, 137n16
Lebacqz, Karen, 131n4
Legba: *see* Eshu
Lewinsky, Monica, 48
liberalism, 4, 15, 18–19, 21–22, 25, 32–36, 40–41, 43, 46, 49, 55, 57, 63, 79, 122, 125n2, 127n8
Lincoln Hospital, 91
Lincoln Park, 89–91
Lodge, Henry Cabot, 9
Los Angeles, Calif., 95
love, 17–18, 35, 49–50, 84, 117
Lovin, Robin, 28
Loyola Marymount University, 95
Lucero: *see* Eshu
lucha, la, 31, 62, 74–78, 86–88, 93, 132n14
Luther, Martin, 18

Mahan, Alfred Thayer, 9
Malverde, Jesús, 117–18
Manifest Destiny, 10–13, 15, 49, 79
Martell-Otero, Loida I., 76
Martí, José, x, 117
Matthew, gospel of, ix, 82, 116, 133n19
McCain, John, 34, 57
McCormick Seminary, 90
McIntyre, James, 95
Mendiola, Michael Manuel, 67, 131n4
Merry Maids, 45–46
mestizaje, xii, 68, 74

Metropolitan Club, 9–10
Mexican-American War, 27
Mexico, 13, 27, 79, 100–101, 113,
   117–18, 120–21; Mexican Ameri-
   cans, 27, 30, 35, 68, 73, 95,
   101–3, 111–12, 120
Miami, Fla., 110
Miami Beach, Fla., 103
Míguez Bonino, José, 18, 97
Moab, 115
Moreno Reyes, Mario: *see*
   Cantinflas
Moss Jr., Otis, 129n25
multinational corporations, 11, 18,
   20, 41, 45, 51–53, 79, 125n2

NAFTA, 30, 50, 120–21
National Association of Hispanic
   Journalists, 132n16
National Council of La Raza,
   132n16
Native Americans, 8, 30, 35, 45,
   49, 54, 73–74, 113; Aztecs, 74;
   Chicano/a, 45, 95
Nazism, 15, 120
neoconservatism, 12, 36–37, 39, 41
neoliberalism, 20, 38–39, 45,
   50–53, 58, 92–94, 98, 125n2
nepantla, 72–74, 77, 86–88, 132n13
Nero, emperor, 12
Network of Spiritual Progress, 42
New York City, 6, 89–90, 95
Niebuhr, Reinhold, xi, 5–6, 14–21,
   32, 126nn6–7
Nogales, Ariz., 121
No More Deaths, 121, 139n27
North Carolina, 34
Nuremberg trials, 120

Obama, Barack, 34–35, 56–59,
   101, 129n22
Obatalá, 108–9
Obi, 109
Oggún, 108–9
O'Hare Airport, 134n6

Olofi, 109
Omri, King, 11
orientalism, 11–12, 126n3
orisha, 108
Our Lady Queen of Girls High
   School, 95

Pacific School of Religion, 131n4
pacifism, 25, 92
Palmer Theological Seminary, 43
Palo Mayombe, 108
panopticon, 102–4
Paterson, N.J., 116
Paul, St., 12
Pedro de Urdemalas, 112
Pedro Ordimales: *see* Pedro de
   Urdemalas
Pentecostal, 61, 116
Pepito, 110–11
Peru, 113
Peters, Pete, 37
Philippines, 10–12, 126n4
pietism, 6, 13, 22, 28, 30, 42,
   83–84, 106
Plaskow, Judith, 16
Platt Amendment, 126n7
police brutality, 60, 89–91, 96, 98,
   103, 132n16, 135n8, 137n14
PostAmerican, 55, 60; *see also*
   Sojourners
poverty, 3, 7, 18, 20, 24, 37, 39–40,
   43–47, 50–51, 55, 57, 58, 60,
   72, 78, 86, 90, 92–93, 95–96,
   98, 102, 109–10, 113, 117–18,
   128n12, 134n2, 135n7, 136n12,
   138n18
praxis, 4, 7, 21–23, 25–29, 41, 43,
   47, 51, 61–62, 68, 70–71, 78–79,
   92, 134nn21, 6–7; liberative, xii,
   4, 22–23, 27, 32, 68, 70, 75, 77,
   83–87, 93–94, 96–97, 99, 101,
   105–6, 115, 118–20, 122; orthopraxis, 22, 83, 134n21
preferential option, for the church,
   23; for the empire, 20, 29; for

Hispanics, 72, 100; for order, 17; for the poor and oppressed, 7, 14, 23, 77, 72, 78, 82; for property rights, 30
pride, sin of, 14–16, 19
Primera Iglesia Metodista Hispana, la, 90–91
property rights, 8, 30, 45, 118
Protestant, 6, 10, 29, 47, 96
Puah, 115
Puerto Rico, 10; Puerto Ricans, 89–90, 110–11

Quakers, 120
Quwi, 109–10, 139n23

racial and ethnic reconciliation, 36–39, 54, 126n7
racism, 3, 5, 7–9, 14–16, 18, 20, 23–24, 29, 31, 36–39, 46, 57, 53, 59, 80–83, 98, 120, 128n12, 133n19
Ramsey, Paul, 17
Rauschenbusch, Walter, xi, 5–14, 32, 126nn2, 4–5
Rawls, John, 17
realism, 14, 17–18, 20
Reagan, Ronald, 36
Rehnquist, William, 38
Religious Center, 35–36, 39–40, 61–62, 128n10
Religious Left, 33–36, 40–43, 49, 54, 61–62, 128n10
Religious Right, 33–42, 49, 55, 61–62
Republican Party, 33, 42, 128n1
Richardson, Bill, 57–58
Riverside Church, 95–96, 100
Riverside Manifesto, 95–96, 134n5
Robertson, Pat, 36
Robespierre, Maximilien, 122
Robin Hood, 117
Rochester, N.Y., 134n6
Rochester Symphony Orchestra, 134n6

Rochester Theological Seminary, 8
Rodríguez, José David, 76
Romans, book of, 94
Roosevelt, Franklin, 128n3
Roosevelt, Theodore, 9, 128n3

Sague, Consuelo, 130n34
Said, Edward W., 126n3
Saint Basil Church, 95
Saiving, Valerie, 16
salvation, 47, 68, 82, 84, 86, 101, 105, 113, 123, 133n19; for Hispanics, 24–25, 33, 36, 62–63, 71, 81, 133n20; personal, 43–44, 56, 128n12
Samson, 115
Samuel, books of, 115
sanctuary movement, 26, 60–61, 119–20, 130nn31–32, 139n27
San Diego, Calif., 121
Santería, 108
Satan, 10, 12, 20, 37, 85, 91, 105, 115–16, 139n26
Saturn, god, 122
Saudi Arabia, 19
Schlafly, Phyllis, 38
Scott, James C., 106
Seattle, Wash., 73
segregation, 15–16, 24–26, 40, 103–4, 135n7, 138nn18–19
sexism, 23, 57, 83, 71, 75, 103, 116–17, 126n6, 139nn21–22
Shiphrah, 115
Sider, Ronald J., 36, 42–49, 51, 53–54, 56, 59–60, 128nn10, 12, 129n14
sin, 7, 14, 16, 19, 29, 43, 45, 47, 53–54, 81–82, 84, 86, 104, 117
Sioux City, Iowa, 73
Sisera, 115
slavery, 24, 29, 35, 49, 52, 80
social gospel, 6, 9, 14, 126n5
socialism, 6–7, 15, 45
Socialist Party, 15
social order (law and order), 7, 9,

12, 15–18, 20, 30, 40–41, 52,
59, 94, 97, 101, 105, 113, 115;
disruption of, 16–17, 94, 96–105,
107–8, 114, 121; global, 15, 17,
19, 38, 55, 125n2
Society of Christian Ethics, xii, 4,
67–69
Sojourners, 54–55, 60–61
Solomon, King, 115
Sonoran desert, 80
Sotomayor, Sonia, 102
South America, 13, 109; *see also*
Latin America
Southern Baptist Convention, 41
Southside Presbyterian Church,
139n27
Spanish-American War, 10–13
Spirit, Holy, 116–17
Stevens Arroyo, Antonio M., 131n9
Strong, Josiah, 13
*Structures of Nations and Empire,
The*, 18
Students for a Democratic Society,
90
Supreme Court, 102, 138n18

Tarango, Yolanda, 130n33
Teatro Campesino, el, 113, 139n25
Temple University, 131n5
Teutoburg Forest, 8
Teutons, 8–9, 126n2
Texas, 24, 73, 90, 121
Texas Rangers, 35
theology, 43, 45, 67, 76, 133n20;
crusade, 56; evangelical, 46; fem-
inist, 131n3; Hispanic, 76, 78,
96, 131n3; liberative, 25, 60, 96,
127n11; narrative, 21; neoconser-
vative (empire), 36, 43–44, 56;
urban, 78; wholistic, 43
Theology for the Social Gospel, A,
126n5
Thistlethwaite, Susan, 16, 126n6
Thomson, John B., 127n11
Tío Antonio, 109

trickster figures, 97, 105–17,
139n21, 139n26
Turner, Victor, 107
Two-Thirds World nations, 19–20,
49–50, 56, 73, 98, 120, 125n2

unemployment: *see* employment
Union Theological Seminary,
131n3
United Farm Workers, 60–61, 95,
139n25
United States, 6, 9, 15, 24, 34, 37,
48–49, 51–53, 55, 61–62, 72–73,
80, 82, 89–90, 95–96, 101, 103,
116–21, 126nn5, 7, 130n31,
133n19, 134n6; Border Patrol,
121; Bureau of Justice Statistics,
132n16; Bureau of Labor Statistics, 136n13; Census Bureau,
34, 135n7, 136n12, 137nn15–16;
Department of Commerce,
138n20; Department of Education, 136n11; as empire, xii,
3–5, 9–13, 15, 17–21, 23, 26–27,
30–36, 38–41, 43–46, 48–60,
62–63, 79, 92–94, 97–98, 100–
101, 107–8, 120, 122, 125n1,
126n7, 128n3; Euroamericans,
3–6, 8, 16–18, 23–24, 26–27,
31–32, 38, 40–41, 46, 48, 50,
54, 57, 60–62, 67, 69–73, 76,
79–81, 83–84, 86–88, 93–94,
96, 104–5, 112, 120, 122,
133nn19–20, 135nn7–9, 136n13,
137nn14–15, 138n18; the South,
7–8, 16, 24–25, 34, 40, 126n1;
southwestern, 24, 27, 29, 73, 80,
95, 112, 117, 119, 121; *see also*
immigration
United States v. Goering, 120
University of Chicago, 131n1

Valdez, Luis Miguel, 139n25
Via Crucis, 78
Vietnam, 19, 55

Viguerie, Richard, 38
Villafañe, Eldin, 67, 131n2, 132n10
virgen de Guadalupe, 113
Vision and Virtue, 22
Vodou, 108

Wake Up, America! 48
Wallace, George, 40
Wallis, Jim, 36, 42, 54–61, 128n10
Walmart, 41
Watergate, 55
West, Traci, 16
Weyrich, Paul, 38

White, Jeremiah, 59
Wilson, Pete, 37
Winant, Howard, 37–38
Wogaman, J. Philip, 55
Wood, Leonard, 10
World War I, 6, 126nn2, 4
World War II, 15, 17, 20

Yemmú, 108
Young Lords, 60, 89–92, 98–99,
    108, 134n1
Young Patriots, 90, 134n2